LAWS AND LEGISLATION

PHARMACEUTICAL PATENTS

ISSUES AND CONSIDERATIONS

Laws and Legislation

Additional books in this series can be found on Nova's website under the Series tab.

Additional E-books in this series can be found on Nova's website under the E-book tab.

Pharmacology - Research, Safety Testing and Regulation

Additional books in this series can be found on Nova's website under the Series tab.

Additional E-books in this series can be found on Nova's website under the E-book tab.

LAWS AND LEGISLATION

PHARMACEUTICAL PATENTS

ISSUES AND CONSIDERATIONS

FLORIAN AERTS
EDITOR

New York

For permission to use material from this book please contact us:
Telephone 631-231-7269; Fax 631-231-8175
Web Site: http://www.novapublishers.com

LIBRARY OF CONGRESS CATALOGING-IN-PUBLICATION DATA

ISBN: 978-1-62618-758-0

Published by Nova Science Publishers, Inc. † New York

CONTENTS

PREFACE

Although brand-name pharmaceutical companies routinely procure patents on their innovative medications, such rights are not self-enforcing. Brand-name firms that wish to enforce their patents against generic competitors must therefore commence litigation in the federal courts. Such litigation ordinarily terminates in either a judgment of infringement, which typically blocks generic competition until such time as the patent expires, or a judgment that the patent is invalid or not infringed, which typically opens the market to generic entry. This book introduces and analyzes innovation and competition policy issues associated with pharmaceutical patent litigation settlements. It begins with a review of pharmaceutical patent litigation procedures under the Hatch-Waxman Act, then introduces the concept of reverse payment settlements, and analyzes the status of reverse payment settlements under antitrust laws, and discusses congressional issues and possible alternatives.

Chapter 1 – Although brand-name pharmaceutical companies routinely procure patents on their innovative medications, such rights are not self-enforcing. Brand-name firms that wish to enforce their patents against generic competitors must therefore commence litigation in the federal courts. Such litigation ordinarily terminates in either a judgment of infringement, which typically blocks generic competition until such time as the patent expires, or a judgment that the patent is invalid or not infringed, which typically opens the market to generic entry.

As with other sorts of commercial litigation, however, the parties to pharmaceutical patent litigation may choose to settle their case. Certain of these settlements have called for the generic firm to neither challenge the brand-name company's patents nor sell a generic version of the patented drug for a period of time. In exchange, the brand-name drug company agrees to compensate the generic firm, often with substantial monetary payments over a number of years. Because the payment flows counterintuitively, from the patent owner to the accused infringer, this compensation has been termed a "reverse" payment.

Commentators have differed markedly in their views of reverse payment settlements. Some observers believe that they are a consequence of the specialized patent litigation procedures established by the Hatch-Waxman Act. Others have concluded that when one competitor pays another not to market its product, such a settlement is anti-competitive and a violation of the antitrust laws.

Since 2003, Congress has required that litigants notify federal antitrust authorities of their pharmaceutical patent settlements. That legislation did not dictate substantive standards for assessing the validity of these agreements under the antitrust law, however. That determination was left to judicial application of general antitrust principles. Facing different factual patterns, some courts have concluded that a particular reverse payment settlement constituted an antitrust violation, while others have upheld the agreement. The Supreme Court agreed to hear a reverse payment settlement case, Federal Trade Commission v. Watson Pharmaceuticals, Inc., on December 7, 2012, and may possibly issue a ruling that provides a nationally uniform judicial approach to these agreements.

Congress possesses a number of alternatives for addressing reverse payment settlements. One possibility is to await further judicial developments. Another option is to regulate the settlement of pharmaceutical patent litigation in some manner. For example, one unenacted proposal from the 112th Congress, H.R. 3995, would have declared that certain reverse payment settlements violate the antitrust laws. Another possibility, proposed by S. 27 in the 112th Congress but not enacted, would establish a presumption of either legality or illegality under the antitrust laws, along with consideration of relevant factors to be weighed by the courts. Still another unenacted proposal from the 112th Congress, S. 1882, would have introduced reforms to the food and drug laws that would have reduced incentives for generic firms to settle with brand-name companies. Any of these, or other proposals, may be revisited by policymakers during the 113th Congress.

Chapter 2 – In combination, patents and regulatory exclusivities provide the fundamental framework of intellectual property incentives for pharmaceutical innovation in the United States. Patents, which are administered by the United States Patent and Trademark Office (USPTO), provide their owner with the ability to exclude others from practicing the claimed invention for a limited time. In contrast, regulatory exclusivities are administered by the Food and Drug Administration (FDA). Alternatively known as marketing exclusivities, data exclusivities, or data protection, regulatory exclusivities establish a period of time during which the FDA affords an approved drug protection from competing applications for marketing approval.

Although patents and regulatory exclusivities are separate entitlements that are administered by different federal administrative agencies and that depend upon distinct criteria, they both create proprietary rights in pharmaceutical and biologics innovation. These rights allow innovators to receive a return on the expenditure of resources leading to a discovery. Once these proprietary interests expire, the marketplace for that drug is open to generic or follow-on competition.

Congressional interest in promoting both innovation and competition in the pharmaceutical industry has focused attention on both patents and regulatory exclusivities. For example, the 112th Congress proposed but did not enact the Modernizing Our Drug and Diagnostics Evaluation and Regulatory Network Cures Act, or MODDERN Cures Act (H.R. 3497). This bill confronted policy makers with a debate previously conducted by legal academics over the relative role of patents and regulatory exclusivities in promoting pharmaceutical and biotechnology R&D. In addition, the Obama Administration has proposed a reduction in the regulatory exclusivity offered to brand-name biologic drugs to seven years, down from the 12 years incorporated in the Biologics Price Competition and Innovation Act of 2009 (enacted as Title VII of the Patient Protection and Affordable Care Act). Controversy has surrounded the award of regulatory exclusivities to colchicine, an ancient remedy for gout that was subject to the FDA's Unapproved Drugs Initiative.

International agreements require each World Trade Organization (WTO) member state to treat all patented inventions in the same manner. This rule seemingly prohibits discrimination both against and in favor of patents on drugs as compared to other technologies. As a result, regulatory exclusivities provide Congress with a more flexible option for stimulating specific sorts of desirable private activity than do patents. The WTO Agreements, as well as certain Free Trade Agreements to which the United States is a signatory, also obligate nations to provide some manner of protection to pharmaceutical test data. Discussion over the inclusion of regulatory exclusivity requirements within the Trans-Pacific Partnership (TPP) is ongoing.

Chapter 3 – Concerns over the availability of affordable health care have focused national attention upon patents and other intellectual property rights awarded to pharmaceutical firms. Legislation that was introduced before, but not enacted by, the 112th Congress proposed amendments to the Hatch-Waxman Act, legislation dating from 1984 that governs intellectual property rights in pharmaceuticals and other regulated products. Recent rulings from the federal judiciary regarding the Hatch-Waxman Act may be pertinent to future congressional consideration of that statute. Both the judicial holdings, as well as possible legislative changes to the Hatch-Waxman Act, potentially affect the availability of both brand-name and generic drugs in the United States.

The Hatch-Waxman Act includes two core provisions that impact the enforcement of patent rights by brand-name firms against generic pharmaceutical companies. 35 U.S.C. §271(e)(1) creates a statutory "safe harbor" that exempts firms from claims of patent infringement based on clinical trials and other acts reasonably related to seeking marketing approval from the Food and Drug Administration (FDA). The explicit wording of that statute does not preclude activities that occur after the receipt of FDA marketing approval from the "safe harbor." Two recent opinions from the U.S. Court of Appeals for the Federal Circuit are arguably in tension over whether post-approval acts are exempted from infringement, however.

A second provision, 35 U.S.C. §271(e)(2), allows a brand-name drug company to enforce its patents against a potential generic competitor at such time that the generic firm files an application—a so-called Abbreviated New Drug Application (ANDA)—with the FDA seeking marketing approval. Although courts have stated that this litigation may only be based upon patents identified to the FDA and listed in the so-called "Orange Book," the express wording of the statute does not appear to impose this requirement. This issue has yet to be conclusively resolved in the courts.

Should Congress conclude that the current situation with respect to 35 U.S.C. §271(e) is satisfactory, no action need be taken. If Congress wishes to intervene, however, then some options present themselves. Congress could stipulate whether 35 U.S.C. §271(e)(1) applies to acts that occur following the award of FDA marketing approval or not. Congress could also explicitly state whether 35 U.S.C. §271(e)(2) establishes a cause of action for infringement of patents that have not been listed in the Orange Book.

Chapter 4 – Congressional interest in health-related issues has refocused attention on legislative efforts to provide both new as well as lower-cost pharmaceuticals for the marketplace. P.L. 98-417, the Drug Price Competition and Patent Term Restoration Act of 1984 (commonly known as the Hatch-Waxman Act), made significant changes to the patent laws as they apply to pharmaceutical products in an attempt to balance the need for innovative new drugs and the availability of less expensive generic products. The act created several practices intended to facilitate the marketing of generic drugs while permitting brand name companies to recover a portion of their intellectual property rights lost during the pharmaceutical approval process. Twenty-five years later, the impact of the act on the pharmaceutical industry may have implications for current congressional efforts to facilitate the development of new, inventive products while reducing costs to consumers.

Prior to the implementation of the Hatch-Waxman Act, 35% of top-selling drugs had generic competitors after patent expiration; now almost all do. The Generic Pharmaceutical Association points out that of 12,751 drugs listed in the Orange Book, 10,072 have generic substitutes available to consumers. Concurrently, the time to market for these generic products has decreased substantially. According to the Congressional Budget Office, in 1984 the average time between the expiration of a patent on a brand name drug and the availability of a generic was three years. Today, upon FDA approval a generic may be introduced immediately after patents on the innovator drug expire as companies are permitted to undertake clinical testing during the time period associated patents are in force. In cases where the generic manufacturer is the patent holder, a substitute drug may be brought to market before the patent expires.

Industry support for pharmaceutical research and development has grown since the passage of the legislation although some recent figures indicate reduced R&D spending by several companies. In the absence of the research, development, and testing performed by the brand name pharmaceutical companies, generic drugs would not exist. The provisions of the Hatch-Waxman Act permit the generic industry to rely on information generated and financed by the brand name companies to obtain approval for their product by the FDA. However, the pharmaceutical industry today differs significantly from what it was in the early 1980s when the legislation was enacted. The cost of developing a drug has doubled, as has the number of clinical trials necessary to file a new drug application. The number of participants required for these trials has tripled. As the rate of return on investments in a new drug declined 12%, manufacturers often spend R&D dollars on developing improved versions of, or new delivery methods for an existing product.

Many experts agree that the Drug Price Competition and Patent Term Restoration Act has had a significant effect on the availability of generic substitutes for brand name drugs. Yet, congressional concerns remain whether or not the balance inherent in the act remains appropriate over 25 years later.

In: Pharmaceutical Patents
Editor: Florian Aerts

ISBN: 978-1-62618-758-0

Chapter1

Pharmaceutical Patent Settlements: Issues in Innovation and Competitiveness*

John R. Thomas

Summary

Although brand-name pharmaceutical companies routinely procure patents on their innovative medications, such rights are not self-enforcing. Brand-name firms that wish to enforce their patents against generic competitors must therefore commence litigation in the federal courts. Such litigation ordinarily terminates in either a judgment of infringement, which typically blocks generic competition until such time as the patent expires, or a judgment that the patent is invalid or not infringed, which typically opens the market to generic entry.

As with other sorts of commercial litigation, however, the parties to pharmaceutical patent litigation may choose to settle their case. Certain of these settlements have called for the generic firm to neither challenge the brand-name company's patents nor sell a generic version of the patented drug for a period of time. In exchange, the brand-name drug company agrees to compensate the generic firm, often with substantial monetary payments over a number of years. Because the payment flows

---

* This is an edited, reformatted and augmented version of a Congressional Research Service publication, CRS Report for Congress R42960, from www.crs.gov, prepared for Members and Committees of Congress, dated February 15, 2013.

counterintuitively, from the patent owner to the accused infringer, this compensation has been termed a "reverse" payment.

Commentators have differed markedly in their views of reverse payment settlements. Some observers believe that they are a consequence of the specialized patent litigation procedures established by the Hatch-Waxman Act. Others have concluded that when one competitor pays another not to market its product, such a settlement is anti-competitive and a violation of the antitrust laws.

Since 2003, Congress has required that litigants notify federal antitrust authorities of their pharmaceutical patent settlements. That legislation did not dictate substantive standards for assessing the validity of these agreements under the antitrust law, however. That determination was left to judicial application of general antitrust principles. Facing different factual patterns, some courts have concluded that a particular reverse payment settlement constituted an antitrust violation, while others have upheld the agreement. The Supreme Court agreed to hear a reverse payment settlement case, Federal Trade Commission v. Watson Pharmaceuticals, Inc., on December 7, 2012, and may possibly issue a ruling that provides a nationally uniform judicial approach to these agreements.

Congress possesses a number of alternatives for addressing reverse payment settlements. One possibility is to await further judicial developments. Another option is to regulate the settlement of pharmaceutical patent litigation in some manner. For example, one unenacted proposal from the 112th Congress, H.R. 3995, would have declared that certain reverse payment settlements violate the antitrust laws. Another possibility, proposed by S. 27 in the 112th Congress but not enacted, would establish a presumption of either legality or illegality under the antitrust laws, along with consideration of relevant factors to be weighed by the courts. Still another unenacted proposal from the 112th Congress, S. 1882, would have introduced reforms to the food and drug laws that would have reduced incentives for generic firms to settle with brand-name companies. Any of these, or other proposals, may be revisited by policymakers during the 113th Congress.

INTRODUCTION

The increasing costs of health care have focused congressional attention upon both the development and public availability of prescription drugs. Congress has long recognized that the patent system has an important role to play in the pharmaceutical industry in each respect. The Drug Price Competition and Patent Term Restoration Act of 1984,[1] commonly known as the Hatch-Waxman Act, in part reformed both the patent and food and drug laws in order to balance incentives for innovation and competition within the pharmaceutical industry.[2]

Recently, congressional attention has been directed towards one aspect of the patent system, the settlement of pharmaceutical patent litigation. Although brand-name pharmaceutical companies commonly procure patents on their innovative products and processes, such rights are not self-enforcing. If a brand-name drug company wishes to enforce its patents against generic competitors, it must pursue litigation in the federal courts. Such litigation ordinarily terminates in either a judgment of infringement, which typically blocks generic competition until such time as the patent expires, or a judgment that the patent is invalid or not infringed, which typically opens the market to generic entry.

As with other sorts of commercial litigation, however, the parties to pharmaceutical patent litigation may choose to settle their case. Certain of these settlements call for the generic firm to neither challenge the brand-name company's patents nor sell a generic version of the patented drug. In exchange, the brand-name drug company agrees to make cash payments to the generic firm. This compensation has been termed an "exclusion" or "exit" payment or, because the payment flows counterintuitively, from the patent proprietor to the accused infringer, a "reverse" payment."[3] Some observers have also termed these settlements as "pay-for-delay" agreements.[4]

Commentators differ markedly in their views of reverse payment settlements. Some observers believe that they result from the specialized patent litigation procedures established by the Hatch-Waxman Act.[5] Others conclude that when one competitor pays another not to market its product, such a settlement is anti-competitive and presumptively a violation of the antitrust laws.[6]

Since 2003, Congress has required that litigants notify federal antitrust authorities of their pharmaceutical patent settlements.[7] To date, Congress has not stipulated substantive standards for assessing the validity of these agreements under the antitrust law, however. That determination was left to judicial application of general antitrust principles. Uniformity of results has not been a hallmark of this line of cases. Facing different factual patterns, some courts have concluded that a particular reverse payment settlement constituted an antitrust violation, while others have upheld the agreement.[8] The announcement of the Supreme Court on December 7, 2012, that it would hear argument in the case of *Federal Trade Commission v. Watson*

Pharmaceuticals, Inc.[9] may potentially lead to a uniform standard of antitrust treatment of reverse payment settlements by the judiciary.

A number of bills were introduced in the 112th Congress pertaining to reverse payment settlements although none were enacted. The Preserve Access to Affordable Generics Act (S. 27) would have created a rebuttable presumption that certain reverse payment settlements were illegal. The Protecting Consumer Access to Generic Drugs Act of 2012 (H.R. 3995) would have rendered certain reverse payment settlements illegal *per se*. Finally, the FAIR Generics Act (S. 1882) would have introduced reforms to the Hatch-Waxman Act that would have reduced incentives for generic firms to settle with brand-name companies. Some policymakers may wish to revisit these legislative proposals during the 113th Congress.

This report introduces and analyzes innovation and competition policy issues associated with pharmaceutical patent litigation settlements. It begins with a review of pharmaceutical patent litigation procedures under the Hatch-Waxman Act. The report then introduces the concept of reverse payment settlements. Next, the report analyzes the status of reverse payment settlements under the antitrust laws. The report closes with a summary of congressional issues and possible alternatives.

PATENT DISPUTES UNDER THE HATCH-WAXMAN ACT

Patent Fundamentals

Inventors must prepare and submit applications to the U.S. Patent and Trademark Office (USPTO) if they wish to obtain patent protection.[10] USPTO officials, known as examiners, then assess whether the application merits the award of a patent.[11] A patent application must include a specification that so completely describes the invention that skilled artisans are able to practice it without undue experimentation. Applicants must also draft at least one claim that particularly points out and distinctly claims the subject matter that they regard as their invention.[12]

While reviewing a submitted application, the examiner will determine whether the claimed invention fulfills certain substantive standards set by the patent statute. Two of the most important patentability criteria are novelty and nonobviousness. To be judged novel, the claimed invention must not be fully anticipated by a prior patent, publication, or other knowledge within the public domain.[13] The sum of these earlier materials, which document state-of-the-art knowledge that is accessible to the public, is termed the "prior art." To meet the standard of nonobviousness, an invention must not have been readily within the ordinary skills of a competent artisan based upon the teachings of the prior art.[14]

If the USPTO allows the application to issue as a granted patent, the owner or owners of the patent obtain the right to exclude others from making, using, selling, offering to sell or importing into the United States the claimed invention.[15] The term of the patent is ordinarily set at twenty years from the date the patent application was filed.[16] Patent title therefore provides inventors with limited periods of exclusivity in which they may practice their inventions, or license others to do so. The grant of a patent permits inventors to receive a return on the expenditure of resources leading to the discovery, often by charging a higher price than would prevail in a competitive market. In the pharmaceutical industry, for example, the introduction of generic competition often results in the availability of lower-cost substitutes for the innovative product.

A patent proprietor bears responsibility for monitoring its competitors to determine whether they are using the patented invention. Patent owners who wish to compel others to observe their intellectual property rights must often commence litigation in the federal district courts.

FDA Approval Procedures

Although the award of a patent claiming a pharmaceutical provides its owner with a proprietary interest in that product, it does not actually allow the owner to distribute that product to the public. Permission from the FDA must first be obtained. In order to obtain FDA marketing approval, the developer of a new drug must demonstrate that the product is safe and effective. This showing typically requires the drug's sponsor to conduct both preclinical and clinical investigations. In deciding whether to issue marketing approval or not, the FDA evaluates the test data that the sponsor submits in a so-called New Drug Application (NDA).[17]

Prior to the enactment of the Hatch-Waxman Act, the federal food and drug law contained no separate provisions addressing marketing approval for independent generic versions of drugs that had previously been approved by the FDA. The result was that a would-be generic drug manufacturer had to file its own NDA in order to sell its product. Some generic manufacturers could rely on published scientific literature demonstrating the safety and efficacy of the drug by submitting a so-called "paper NDA." Because these sorts of studies were not available for all drugs, however, not all generic firms could file a paper NDA.

Further, at times the FDA requested additional studies to address safety and efficacy questions that arose from experience with the drug following its initial approval. The result was that some generic manufacturers were forced to prove once more that a particular drug was safe and effective, even though their products were chemically identical to those of previously approved pharmaceuticals.[18]

Some commentators believed that the approval of a generic drug was a needlessly costly, duplicative, and time-consuming process. These observers noted that although patents on important drugs had expired, manufacturers were not moving to introduce generic equivalents for these products due to the level of resource expenditure required to obtain FDA marketing approval.[19]

In response to these concerns, Congress enacted the Hatch-Waxman Act, a complex statute that sought compromise between brand-name and generic pharmaceutical companies.[20] Its provisions included the creation of an expedited marketing approval pathway for generic drugs termed an Abbreviated New Drug Application, or ANDA. An ANDA allows an independent generic applicant to obtain marketing approval by demonstrating that the proposed product is bioequivalent to an approved pioneer drug, without providing evidence of safety and effectiveness from clinical data or from the scientific literature. The availability of ANDAs often allows a generic manufacturer to avoid the costs and delays associated with filing a full-fledged NDA. They may also allow an independent generic manufacturer, in many cases, to place its FDA-approved bioequivalent drug on the market as soon as any relevant patents expire.[21]

As part of the balance struck between brand-name and generic firms, Congress also provided patent proprietors with a means for restoring a portion of the patent term that had been lost while awaiting FDA approval. The maximum extension period is capped at a five-year extension period, or a total effective patent term after the extension of not more than 14 years. The scope of rights during the period of extension is generally limited to the use approved for the product that subjected it to regulatory delay.

This period of patent term extension is intended to compensate brand-name firms for the generic drug industry's reliance upon the proprietary pre-clinical and clinical data they have generated, most often at considerable expense to themselves.[22]

Resolution of Patent Disputes

During its development of accelerated marketing approval procedures for generic drugs, Congress recognized that the brand-name pharmaceutical firm may be the proprietor of one or more patents directed towards that drug product. These patents might be infringed by a product described by a generic firm's ANDA or in the event that product is approved by the FDA and sold in the marketplace. The Hatch-Waxman Act therefore established special procedures for resolving patent disputes in connection with applications for marketing generic drugs.[23]

In particular, the Hatch-Waxman Act states that each NDA applicant "shall file" a list of patents that the applicant believes would be infringed if a generic drug were marketed prior to the expiration of these patents.[24] The FDA then lists these patents in a publication titled *Approved Drug Products with Therapeutic Equivalence Evaluations*, which is more commonly known as the "Orange Book."[25] Would-be manufacturers of generic drugs must then engage in a specialized certification procedure with respect to Orange Book-listed patents. An ANDA applicant must state its views with respect to each Orange Book-listed patent associated with the drug it seeks to market. Four possibilities exist:

1) that the brand-name firm has not filed any patent information with respect to that drug;
2) that the patent has already expired;
3) that the generic company agrees not to market until the date on which the patent will expire; or
4) that the patent is invalid or will not be infringed by the manufacture, use, or sale of the drug for which the ANDA is submitted.[26]

These certifications are respectively termed paragraph I, II, III, and IV certifications. An ANDA certified under paragraphs I or II is approved immediately after meeting all applicable regulatory and scientific requirements. An independent generic firm that files an ANDA including a paragraph III certification must, even after meeting pertinent regulatory and scientific requirements, wait for approval until the brand-name drug's listed patent expires.[27]

The filing of an ANDA with a paragraph IV certification constitutes a "somewhat artificial" act of patent infringement under the Hatch-Waxman Act.[28] The act requires the independent generic applicant to notify the proprietor of the patents that are the subject of a paragraph IV certification. The patent owner may then commence patent infringement litigation against that applicant.[29]

Generic Exclusivity

In order to encourage challenges of pharmaceutical patents, the Hatch-Waxman Act provides prospective manufacturers of generic pharmaceuticals with a potential reward. That reward consists of a 180-day exclusivity period awarded to the first ANDA applicant to file a paragraph IV certification.[30] Once a first ANDA with a paragraph IV certification has been filed, the FDA cannot issue marketing approval to a subsequent ANDA with a paragraph IV certification on the same drug product for 180 days. Because market prices could drop considerably following the entry of additional generic competition, the first paragraph IV ANDA applicant may potentially obtain more handsome profits than subsequent market entrants—thereby stimulating patent challenges in the first instance.[31]

Following 2003 amendments to the Hatch-Waxman Act,[32] in some circumstances a first paragraph IV ANDA applicant may lose its entitlement to the 180-day generic exclusivity period. The Medicare Prescription Drug, Improvement, and Modernization Act (MMA) established a number of "forfeiture events" that, if triggered, result in a relinquishment of generic exclusivity. Among the forfeiture events are: (1) failure to market its product promptly; (2) failure to obtain FDA approval to market the generic drug in a reasonably timely manner; and (3) all of the certified patents that entitled the applicant to the 180-day generic exclusivity period have expired. The possibility of forfeiture was intended "to prevent the practice of 'parking' the exclusivity period and to force generic manufacturers to market promptly."[33]

Fundamentals of Reverse Payment Settlements

As discussed previously, a generic firm's filing of a paragraph IV ANDA may result in a patent infringement suit brought by a brand-name drug company. In such litigation, if the NDA holder demonstrates that the independent generic firm's proposed product would violate its patents, then the court will ordinarily issue an injunction that prevents the generic drug company from marketing that product. That injunction will expire on the same date as the NDA holder's patents. Independent generic drug companies commonly amend their ANDAs in this event, replacing their paragraph IV certifications with paragraph III certifications.[34]

On the other hand, the courts may decide in favor of the independent generic firm. The court may conclude that the generic firm's proposed product does not infringe the asserted patents, or that the asserted patents are invalid or unenforceable. In this circumstance, the independent generic firm may launch its product once the FDA has finally approved its ANDA.[35]

In addition to the issuance of final judgment in favor of either the brand-name drug company or generic firm, another resolution of pharmaceutical patent litigation is possible. This legal situation led to a number of cases with varying details, but a common core fact pattern. Upon filing a paragraph IV ANDA, a generic firm would be sued for patent infringement as provided by the Hatch-Waxman Act. The NDA holder and generic applicant would then settle their dispute. The settlement would call for the generic firm to neither challenge the patent nor produce a generic version of the patented drug, for a period of time up to the remaining term of the patent. In exchange, the NDA holder would agree to compensate the ANDA applicant, often with substantial monetary payments over a number of years.[36]

Opinions about the effects of reverse payment settlements upon social welfare have varied. Some commentators believe that such settlements are anticompetitive. They believe that many of these agreements may amount to no more than two firms colluding in order to restrict output and share patent-based profits. Such settlements are also said to eliminate the possibility of a judicial holding of patent invalidity, which may open the market to generic competition and benefit consumers.[37]

On the other hand, some commentators have found nothing inherently troublesome about reverse payment settlements. Among their observations is that there is a general judicial policy in favor of promoting settlement.[38] Settlements can allow the parties to avoid the expenses of litigation,[39] achieve a resolution to the dispute in a timely manner, and avoid the risk of an uncertain result in the courtroom. The settlement of litigation further serves the goal of resolving disputes in a peaceful manner, and also preserves scarce judicial resources.[40] Second, any settlement of litigation between rational actors necessarily involves an exchange of benefits and obligations. As Judge Richard Posner has explained:

> *[A]ny* settlement agreement can be characterized as involving "compensation" to the defendant, who would not settle unless he had

> something to show for the settlement. If any settlement agreement is thus to be classified as involving a forbidden "reverse payment," we shall have no more patent settlements.[41]

Third, certain reverse payment settlements have allowed for the introduction of generic competition prior to the date the relevant patent expires. It is possible, for example, for the brand-name and generic firms to divide the remaining patent term between them, with the generic firm being allowed to market a competing product prior to the running of the full patent term. Such agreements may potentially benefit consumers, certainly in comparison to a judgment that the patent is not invalid and infringed.[42]

Finally, the dispute settlement procedures established by the Hatch-Waxman Act may themselves promote the use of reverse payment settlements in pharmaceutical patent litigation. In patent litigation outside the Hatch-Waxman Act context, the accused infringer is ordinarily using or marketing the patented technology.

A judicial finding of infringement would expose the accused infringer to an injunction, along with damages awarded for past uses and sales. As a result, the accused infringer may well be willing to compensate the patent proprietor in order to avoid the risk of such a holding.[43]

Some observers believe that the structure of the Hatch-Waxman Act alters the traditional balance of risks between the plaintiff-patentee and accused infringer. As explained by one federal district court:

> [I]n creating an artificial act of infringement (the ANDA IV filing), the Hatch-Waxman Amendments grant generic manufacturers standing to mount a validity challenge without incurring the cost of entry or risking enormous damages flowing from infringing commercial sales.... Because of the Hatch-Waxman scheme, [the generic firm's] exposure in the patent litigation was limited to litigation costs, but its upside–exclusive generic sales–was immense. The patent holder, however, has no corresponding upside, as there are no infringement damages to collect, but has an enormous downside–losing the patent.[44]

As a result, some commentators believe that it is entirely predictable that the unique procedures of the Hatch-Waxman Act have resulted in the new phenomenon of reverse payment settlements.[45]

At the present time, congressional action on pharmaceutical patent litigation settlements has been limited.

In the 2003 Medicare Prescription Drug, Improvement, and Modernization Act (MMA),[46] Congress mandated that the Department of Justice (DOJ) and the Federal Trade Commission (FTC) receive copies of certain patent settlements agreements in the pharmaceutical field. The filing requirement applies to agreements executed on or after January 7, 2004, between an ANDA applicant, on one hand, and either the NDA holder or an owner of an Orange Book-listed patent, on the other.[47]

Such agreements trigger the statutory notification requirement if they relate to one of three topics:

1) The manufacture, marketing, or sale of the brand-name drug that is the listed drug in the ANDA;
2) The manufacture, marketing, or sale of the generic drug for which the ANDA was submitted; or
3) The 180-day generic exclusivity period as it applies to that ANDA, or to another ANDA filed with respect to the same brand-name drug.[48]

The MMA stipulates that certain agreements are not subject to this filing requirement. In particular, agreements that solely consist of purchase orders for raw materials, equipment and facility contracts, employment or consulting contracts, or packaging and labeling contracts do not need to be submitted to the DOJ or FTC.[49]

The FTC reported that during FY2012 (October 1, 2011, to September 30, 2012), the agency received "140 final resolutions of patent disputes between a brand and a generic, of which 40 settlements may involve pay-for-delay payments."[50]

Although the MMA imposed a filing obligation upon certain patent settlements between pharmaceutical firms, that legislation did not set substantive standards as to the validity of these agreements. Both prior and subsequent to congressional enactment of the MMA, however, various government and private actors asserted that certain reverse payment settlements violated the antitrust laws.

In order to resolve these claims, different courts applied general principles of antitrust law. Facing different factual patterns, the courts ultimately reached varying results. After introducing the basic concepts of antitrust law, this report next reviews several judicial opinions that address reverse payment settlements.

Antitrust Implications of Reverse Payment Settlements

General Antitrust Standards

The primary legal mechanism for addressing conduct alleged to be anti-competitive—including reverse payment settlements—consists of the antitrust laws. The antitrust laws are comprised of the Sherman Act, the Clayton Act, the Federal Trade Commission Act, and other federal and state statutes that prohibit certain kinds of anticompetitive economic conduct. Although a complete review of the antitrust laws exceeds the scope of this report, other sources provide more information for the interested reader.[51]

Section 1 of the Sherman Act declares "[e]very contract, combination in the form of trust or otherwise, or conspiracy, in restraint of trade ... to be illegal." The courts have long interpreted this language as applying only to unreasonable restraints of trade. The determination of whether particular conduct amounts to an unreasonable restraint of trade is commonly conducted under the "rule of reason." Under this approach, "the finder of fact must decide whether the questioned practice imposes an unreasonable restraint on competition, taking into account a variety of factors, including specific information about the relevant business, its condition before and after the restraint was imposed, and the restraint's history, nature, and effect."[52] The rule of reason essentially calls upon courts to reach a judgment of reasonableness by balancing the anticompetitive consequences of a challenged practice against its business justifications and potentially procompetitive impact.[53]

Other sorts of restraints are deemed unlawful *per se*. Per se illegality is appropriate "[o]nce experience with a particular kind of restraint enables the Court to predict with confidence that the rule of reason will condemn it." The Supreme Court has explained that "there are certain agreements or practices which because of their pernicious effect on competition and lack of any redeeming virtue are conclusively presumed to be unreasonable and therefore illegal without elaborate inquiry as to the precise harm they have caused or the business excuse for their use."[54] Among the practices that have been judged per se violations are price fixing, group boycotts, and market division.[55]

In some circumstances, courts apply an antitrust standard that falls between the *per se* illegality standard and the rule of reason. The so-called "quick look" or "truncated rule of reason" approach applies when the plaintiff demonstrates that the defendant has engaged in practices similar to those previously held to be subject to *per se* treatment. In these circumstances, the defendant must then demonstrate that the practice has pro-competitive justifications in order to avoid liability for an antitrust violation.[56]

Judicial Approaches to Reverse Payment Settlements

The courts have differed in their antitrust approaches to reverse payment settlements in pharmaceutical patent litigation.[57] The first two appellate courts to address this issue, from the District of Columbia and Sixth Circuits, subjected such agreements to strict antitrust scrutiny.[58] The Sixth Circuit opinion in *In re Cardizem CD Antitrust Litigation* is representative of this approach.[59] There the Court of Appeals held that a reverse payment settlement agreement between Hoescht Marion Roussel Inc. and Andrx Pharmaceuticals was *per se* invalid. The Sixth Circuit reasoned that the HMR-Andrx agreement was appropriately classified as a so-called horizontal agreement; that is to say, a restraint of trade involving businesses at the same level of competition. Such agreements had long been classified as antitrust violation *per se*, the Court of Appeals explained.

Despite this early precedent, three subsequent Courts of Appeals to consider the matter—from the Second, Eleventh, and Federal Circuits—reached a different result, ruling that reverse payment settlements were permissible so long as they do not authorize arrangements that exceed the scope of the patent.[60] One representative case, *Valley Drug Co. v. Geneva Pharmaceuticals, Inc.*,[61] involved agreements Abbott Laboratories reached with two different generic firms, Zenith Goldline Pharmaceuticals and Geneva Pharmaceuticals. At trial, the district court held that the two settlement agreements constituted a horizontal market allocation that was *per se* illegal under the Sherman Act. The Eleventh Circuit reversed on appeal, concluding that the standard of *per se* illegality was "premature" and inappropriate. Instead, the Court of Appeals remanded the matter for a determination of whether any part of the agreement went beyond the protections afforded by the brand-name firm's patent and, if so, to apply antitrust scrutiny only to those portions of the agreement. Under this "scope of the patent" approach, reverse payment settlements are permitted so long as (1) the commercial arrangement dictated by the settlement does not extend beyond the scope of the patent; (2) the patent holder's claim of infringement was not objectively baseless; and (3) the patent was not obtained by defrauding the USPTO.

On July 16, 2012, the Court of Appeals for the Third Circuit addressed the antitrust status of reverse payments settlements in *K-Dur Antitrust Litigation.*[62]

The Third Circuit rejected the scope of the patent test, explaining that "that test improperly restricts the application of antitrust law and is contrary to the policies underlying the Hatch-Waxman Act and a long line of Supreme Court precedent on patent litigation and competition."[63]

The Third Circuit believed that courts following the scope of the patent test had placed too much weight on the presumption of validity accorded to granted patents.

This presumption was merely a procedural device, not a substantive right of the patent holder, the Court of Appeals explained.[64]

The Court of Appeals also recognized the judicial preference for private settlements, but reasoned that this practice should not displace congressional goals underlying the Hatch-Waxman Act— including the invalidation of improvidently granted patent through litigation.[65] In the view of the Third Circuit, the scope of the patent test essentially prevented antitrust authorities from reviewing settlement agreements involving weak or narrow patents that would not have blocked generic competition. [66] In place of the scope of the patent test, the Third Circuit adopted a "quick rule of reason" test that presumed that reverse payments were anticompetitive. However, the parties to the agreement could rebut that conclusion by demonstrating that the payments were for a purpose other than delayed entry or offered some pro-competitive benefit.[67]

Perhaps due to its awareness of the arguably conflicting standards developed by the lower courts, the Supreme Court agreed to hear a reverse payment settlement case, *Federal Trade Commission v. Watson Pharmaceuticals, Inc.,* on December 7, 2012.[68] The issue presented to the Supreme Court is:

> Whether reverse-payment agreements are *per se* lawful unless the underlying patent litigation was a sham or the patent was obtained by fraud (as the court below held), or instead are presumptively anticompetitive and unlawful (as the Third Circuit has held).

FTC v. Watson Pharmaceuticals, Inc. provides the Supreme Court with the opportunity to issue a ruling that provides a nationally uniform judicial approach to these agreements.

ISSUES AND OBSERVATIONS

In the absence of explicit congressional guidance, the federal courts have applied general principles of antitrust law to reach varying results with respect to pharmaceutical patent litigation settlements. In view of this landscape, several options are available for Congress. One possibility is to await further judicial developments. Supreme Court review of the issue in *FTC v. Watson Pharmaceuticals, Inc.* may potentially resolve the arguable split among the courts of appeal with respect to this issue.

Another option is to regulate the settlement of pharmaceutical patent litigation in some manner. A number of bills were introduced in the 112th Congress pertaining to reverse payment settlements, although none were enacted. These bills, as well as others, may be introduced in the 113th Congress.

The Preserve Access to Affordable Generics Act, S. 27, would have declared that certain reverse payment settlements constitute acts of unfair competition. In particular, that bill would have amended the Federal Trade Commission Act to provide that an agreement "shall be presumed to have anticompetitive effects and be unlawful if—(i) an ANDA filer receives anything of value; and (ii) the ANDA filer agrees to limit or forego research, development, manufacturing, marketing, or sales of the ANDA product for any period of time." That presumption would not apply if the parties to the agreement demonstrated by clear and convincing evidence that the procompetitive benefits of the agreement outweighed the anticompetitive effects of the agreement. S. 27 included a list of factors to be weighed by the courts in such circumstances.[69]

Another bill, The Protecting Consumer Access to Generic Drugs Act of 2012, H.R. 3995, would have declared unlawful "any agreement resolving or settling a patent infringement claim in which—(1) an ANDA filer receives anything of value; and (2) the ANDA filer agrees not to research, develop, manufacture, market, or sell, for any period of time, the drug that is to be manufactured under the ANDA involved and is the subject of the patent infringement claim." However, agreements were not unlawful if the ANDA filer received no more than the right to market the drug prior to the expiration of any intellectual property rights and the waiver of a patent infringement claim for damages based on any earlier marketing of such generic drug.[70]

Finally, the Fair and Immediate Release of Generics Act, S. 1882, would have made a number of changes to the Hatch-Waxman Act in order to discourage reverse payments settlements. In particular, S. 1882 would have granted any generic firm the right to share the 180-day regulatory exclusivity if it wins a patent challenge in the district court or is not sued for patent infringement by the brand company.[71] The legislation would have also obligated generic firms to abide by any deferred entry date agreed to in their settlements with brand-name firms, even if relevant patents were struck down previously.[72] Finally, brand-name firms would have been required to make a decision to enforce their patents within 45 days of being notified of a patent challenge by a generic firm under the Hatch-Waxman Act.[73]

The settlement of pharmaceutical patent litigation forms an important issue because such litigation is itself important to our public health system. Our patient population relies upon brand-name drug companies to develop new medicines, but it also relies upon generic firms to increase access to such medications once they have been developed. The Hatch-Waxman Act provides for patent litigation between these two traditional rivals as a primary vehicle through which these competing demands are mediated. When concluded in a manner that comports with antitrust principles, such settlements may further the public policy goals of encouraging the labors that lead to medical innovation, but also distributing the fruits of those labors to consumers.

End Notes

[1] P L. 84-417, 98 Stat. 1585 (1984).

[2] See CRS Report R41114, The Hatch-Waxman Act: Over a Quarter Century Later, by Wendy H. Schacht and John R. Thomas.

[3] See Alan Devlin & Michael Jacobs, "Anticompetitive Innovation and the Quality of Innovation," 27 Berkeley Technology Law Journal (2012), 1.

[4] See Alyssa L. Brown, "Modest Proposals for a Complex Problem: Patent Misuse and Incremental Changes to the Hatch-Waxman Act as Solutions to the Problem of Reverse Payment Settlements," 41 University of Baltimore Law Review (2012), 583.

[5] See Henry N. Butler and Jeffrey Paul Jarosch, "Policy Reversal on Reverse Payments: Why Courts Should Not Follow the New DOJ Position on Reverse-Payment Settlements of Pharmaceutical Patent Litigation," 96 Iowa Law Review (2010), 57.

[6] See Michael A. Carrier, "Unsettling Drug Patent Settlements: A Framework for Presumptive Illegality," 108 Michigan Law Review (2009), 37.

[7] See Medicare Prescription Drug, Improvement and Modernization Act of 2003, P.L. 108-173, 117 Stat. 2066.

[8] See Michael A. Carrier, "Why the 'Scope of the Patent' Test Cannot Solve the Drug Patent Settlement Problem," 16 Stanford Technology Law Review (2012), 1.

[9] 2012 WL 4758105.

[10] 35 U.S.C. §111.

[11] 35 U.S.C. §131.

[12] 35 U.S.C. §112.

[13] 35 U.S.C. §101.

[14] 35 U.S.C. §103.

[15] 35 U.S.C. §271.

[16] 35 U.S.C. §154(a)(2).

[17] Sec FDA, Drugs: Development & Approval Process (Drugs): How Drugs Are Developed and Approved (April 23, 2010) (available at http://www.fda.gov/drugs/developmentapproval process/howdrugsaredevelopedandapproved/ default.htm).

[18] See Colleen Kelly, "The Balance Between Innovation and Competition: The Hatch-Waxman Act, the 2003 Amendments, and Beyond," 66 Food and Drug Law Journal (2011), 417.

[19] See Matthew Avery, "Continuing Abuse of the Hatch-Waxman Act by Pharmaceutical Patent Holders and the Failure of the 2003 Amendments," 60 Hastings Law Journal (2008), 171.

[20] See Timothy A. Cook, "Pharmaceutical Patent Litigation Settlements: Balancing Patent & Antitrust Policy Through Institutional Choice," 17 Michigan Telecommunications and Technology Law Review (2011), 417.

[21] See Michael R. Herman, "The Stay Dilemma: Examining Brand and Generic Incentives for Delaying the Resolution of Pharmaceutical Patent Litigation," 111 Columbia Law Review (2011), 1788.

[22] See Ann Kotze, "Reining in Patent Term Extensions for Related Pharmaceutical Products Post-Photocure and OrthoMcNeil," 106 Northwestern University Law Review (2012), 1419.

[23] See Linda P. Nussbaum and John D. Radice, "Where Do We Go Now? The Hatch-Waxman Act Twenty-Five Years Later: Successes, Failures, and Prescriptions for the Future," 41 Rutgers Law Journal (2009), 229.

[24] 21 U.S.C. §355(b)(1).

[25] See Ian Hastings, "Dynamic Innovation Inefficiency in Pharmaceutical Patent Settlements," 13 North Carolina Journal of Law & Technology (2011), 31.

[26] 21 U.S.C. §355(j)(2)(A)(vii).

[27] See Emily Michiko Morris, "The Myth of Generic Pharmaceutical Competition Under the Hatch-Waxman Act," 22 Fordham Intellectual Property Media & Entertainment Law Journal (2012), 245.

[28] Eli Lilly & Co. v. Medtronic, 496 U.S. 1047 (1990). The act of infringement is "somewhat artificial" in that the generic drug company has merely filed a paragraph IV ANDA with the FDA, rather than actually making, using, or selling a competing product in the marketplace.

[29] See Morris, supra.

[30] 21 U.S.C. §355(j)(5)(B)(iv).

[31] See Scott Hemphill & Mark A. Lemley, "Earning Exclusivity: Generic Drug Incentives and the Hatch-Waxman Act," 77 Antitrust Law Review (2011), 947.

[32] P.L. 108-173, 117 Stat. 2066.

[33] Brian Porter, "Stopping the Practice of Authorized Generics: Mylan's Effort to Close the Gaping Black Hole in the Hatch-Waxman Act," 22 Journal of Contemporary Health Law and Policy (2005), 177 (citation omitted).

[34] 21 C.F.R. §314.94(a)(12)(viii)(A).

[35] 21 U.S.C. §355(j)(5)(B)(iii).

[36] See C. Scott Hemphill, "Paying for Delay: Pharmaceutical Patent Settlement as a Regulatory Design Problem," 81 New York University Law Review (2006), 1560.

[37] See Carrier, supra.

[38] See Cory J. Ingle, "Reverse Payment Settlements: A Patent Approach for Defending the Argument for Illegality," 7 I/S: A Journal of Law and Policy for the Information Society (2012), 503 (identifying this policy).

[39] The American Intellectual Property Law Association estimated the average cost of patent infringement litigation at $6,018,000 per side for a case worth more than 25 million dollars. See AIPLA Report of the Economic Survey I-153-54 (2011).

[40] See Alex Corona, "Stuck in Neutral: The Future of Reverse Payments Agreements in Hatch-Waxman Litigation," 7 Seton Hall Circuit Review (2010), 201.

[41] Asahi Glass Co. v. Pentech Pharmaceuticals, Inc., 289 F. Supp. 2d 986 (N.D. Ill. 2003) (emphasis in original).

[42] See Corona, supra.

[43] See Scott Bergeson, "A Vaccine Approach to the Reverse Payment Illness," 18 Richmond Journal of Law and Technology (2012), 14.

[44] In re Ciprofloxacin Antirust Litigation, 261 F. Supp. 2d 188, 251 (E.D.N.Y. 2003).

[45] See Thomas F. Cotter, "Antitrust Implications of Patent Settlements Involving Reverse Payments: Defining a Rebuttable Presumption of Illegality in Light of Some Recent Scholarship," 71 Antirust Law Journal (2004), 1069.

[46] P.L. 108-173, 117 Stat. 2066.

[47] MMA, §1112(a)(1).

[48] Ibid.

[49] Ibid. at §1112(c)(1).

[50] See Agreements Filed with the Federal Trade Commission under the Medicare Prescription Drug, Improvement, and Modernization Act of 200, Overview of Agreements Filed in FY2012: A Report by the Bureau of Competition (available at http://www.ftc.gov/os/2013/01/130117mmareport.pdf), 1.

[51] See, e.g., Federal Trade Commission, FTC Guide to the Antitrust Laws (available at http://www.ftc.gov/bc/antitrust/).

[52] State Oil Co. v. Khan, 522 U.S. 3, 10 (1997).

[53] See Meredith Bateman, "In re K-Dur Antitrust Litigation—Reverse Payments: Against Prices, Purchasers, and Policy," 15 Tulane Journal of Technology and Intellectual Property (2012), 293.

[54] Northern Pacific Railroad Co. v. United States, 356 U.S. 1, 5 (1957).

[55] See Leegin Creative Leather Products, Inc. v. PSKS, Inc., 551 U.S. 877 (2007).

[56] See California Dental Association v. FTC, 526 U.S. 756 (1999).

[57] See Einer Elhauge & Alex Krueger, "Solving the Patent Settlement Puzzle," 91 Texas Law Review (2012), 283.

[58] See In re Cardizem CD Antirust Litig., 332 F.3d 896 (6th Cir. 2003); Andrx Pharms. Inc. v. Biovail Corp., 256 F.3d 799 (D.C. Cir. 2001).

[59] 332 F.3d 896 (6th Cir. 2003).

[60] See In re Ciprofloxacin Hydrochloride Antitrust Litigation, 544 F.3d 1323 (Fed. Cir. 2008); Schering-Plough Corp. v. FTC; In re Tamoxifen Citrate Antitrust Litig., 466 F.3d 187 (2d Cir. 2006); Valley Drug Co. v. Geneva Pharms., Inc., 344 F.3d 1294 (11th Cir. 2003).

[61] 344 F.3d 1294 (11th Cir. 2003).

[62] 686 F.3d 197 (3rd Cir. 2012).

[63] Ibid. at 214.

[64] Ibid. at 214-15.

[65] Ibid. at 217-18.

[66] Ibid. at 217.

[67] Ibid. at 218.

[68] 2012 WL 4758105.

[69] S. 27 at §3.

[70] H.R. 3995 at §2.
[71] S. 1882 at §2.
[72] Ibid. at §3(a).
[73] Ibid. at §3(b).

In: Pharmaceutical Patents
Editor: Florian Aerts
ISBN: 978-1-62618-758-0

Chapter 2

THE ROLE OF PATENTS AND REGULATORY EXCLUSIVITIES IN PHARMACEUTICAL INNOVATION*

John R. Thomas

SUMMARY

In combination, patents and regulatory exclusivities provide the fundamental framework of intellectual property incentives for pharmaceutical innovation in the United States. Patents, which are administered by the United States Patent and Trademark Office (USPTO), provide their owner with the ability to exclude others from practicing the claimed invention for a limited time. In contrast, regulatory exclusivities are administered by the Food and Drug Administration (FDA). Alternatively known as marketing exclusivities, data exclusivities, or data protection, regulatory exclusivities establish a period of time during which the FDA affords an approved drug protection from competing applications for marketing approval.

Although patents and regulatory exclusivities are separate entitlements that are administered by different federal administrative agencies and that depend upon distinct criteria, they both create proprietary rights in pharmaceutical and biologics innovation. These

---

* This is an edited, reformatted and augmented version of a Congressional Research Service publication, CRS Report for Congress R42890, from www.crs.gov, prepared for Members and Committees of Congress, dated January 7, 2013.

rights allow innovators to receive a return on the expenditure of resources leading to a discovery. Once these proprietary interests expire, the marketplace for that drug is open to generic or follow-on competition.

Congressional interest in promoting both innovation and competition in the pharmaceutical industry has focused attention on both patents and regulatory exclusivities. For example, the 112th Congress proposed but did not enact the Modernizing Our Drug and Diagnostics Evaluation and Regulatory Network Cures Act, or MODDERN Cures Act (H.R. 3497). This bill confronted policy makers with a debate previously conducted by legal academics over the relative role of patents and regulatory exclusivities in promoting pharmaceutical and biotechnology R&D. In addition, the Obama Administration has proposed a reduction in the regulatory exclusivity offered to brand-name biologic drugs to seven years, down from the 12 years incorporated in the Biologics Price Competition and Innovation Act of 2009 (enacted as Title VII of the Patient Protection and Affordable Care Act). Controversy has surrounded the award of regulatory exclusivities to colchicine, an ancient remedy for gout that was subject to the FDA's Unapproved Drugs Initiative.

International agreements require each World Trade Organization (WTO) member state to treat all patented inventions in the same manner. This rule seemingly prohibits discrimination both against and in favor of patents on drugs as compared to other technologies. As a result, regulatory exclusivities provide Congress with a more flexible option for stimulating specific sorts of desirable private activity than do patents. The WTO Agreements, as well as certain Free Trade Agreements to which the United States is a signatory, also obligate nations to provide some manner of protection to pharmaceutical test data. Discussion over the inclusion of regulatory exclusivity requirements within the Trans-Pacific Partnership (TPP) is ongoing.

BACKGROUND

Congressional interest in stimulating innovation within the pharmaceutical industry has been reflected in legislative activity in the areas of patent law and regulatory exclusivities. In particular, the 112th Congress enacted the Leahy-Smith America Invents Act, P.L. 112-29, which made numerous changes to the nation's patent laws. The 112th Congress also enacted the Food and Drug Administration Safety and Innovation Act, P.L. 112-144. That statute in part addressed so-called pediatric exclusivity and also allowed a "qualified infectious disease product" to be eligible for an extended period of regulatory exclusivity.[1]

In combination, patents and regulatory exclusivities create a relatively complex landscape of intellectual property rights intended to encourage firms to develop and market new drugs. Patents, which are administered by the U.S. Patent and Trademark Office (USPTO), provide firms with exclusive rights to an invention for a limited time in exchange for disclosure of the invention to the public. In contrast, regulatory exclusivities are administered by the Food and Drug Administration (FDA). They consist of a period of time during which the FDA affords an approved drug protection from competing applications for marketing approval.

Although regulatory exclusivities have been available within the healthcare industry for three decades, commentators have raised a number of innovation policy issues in this context. Some observers question the need for innovators to obtain both regulatory exclusivities and patents.[2] Others have expressed concern over the duration of particular regulatory exclusivities.[3] Issues have also arisen with respect to the use of regulatory exclusivities to encourage specific sorts of innovation and with the obligations of other nations to grant regulatory exclusivities in the manner of U.S. law.[4]

This report introduces and analyzes innovation policy issues concerning intellectual property rights in pharmaceutical innovation. It begins with a review of the policy and procedures relating to both patents and regulatory exclusivities. The report then discusses current domestic and international issues that exist at the intersection of these two proprietary rights. The report closes with a summary of congressional issues and potential alternatives.

FUNDAMENTALS OF THE PATENT SYSTEM

The Patent Act of 1952 (also known as the Patent Act) requires innovators to prepare and submit applications to the USPTO if they wish to obtain patent protection.[5] USPTO officials known as examiners then assess whether the application merits the award of a patent. In deciding whether to approve a patent application, a USPTO examiner considers whether the submitted application fully discloses and distinctly claims the invention.[6]

The examiner will also determine whether the invention itself fulfills certain substantive standards set by the patent statute. To be patentable, an invention must consist of a process, machine, manufacture, or composition of matter that is useful, novel, and nonobvious.[7] The requirement of usefulness, or utility, is satisfied if the invention is operable and provides a tangible benefit.[8] To be judged novel, the invention must not be fully anticipated by a prior patent, publication, or other knowledge within the public domain.[9] A nonobvious invention must not have been readily within the ordinary skills of a competent artisan at the time the invention was made.[10]

If the USPTO allows the patent to issue, the patent proprietor obtains the right to exclude others from making, using, selling, offering to sell or importing into the United States the patented invention.[11] The term of the patent is ordinarily set at twenty years from the date the patent application was filed.[12]

Once a patent issues, its proprietor bears responsibility for monitoring its competitors to determine whether they are using the patented invention or not. Patent owners who wish to compel others to observe their intellectual property rights must usually commence litigation in the federal district courts.[13] The U.S. Court of Appeals for the Federal Circuit ("Federal Circuit") possesses exclusive national jurisdiction over all patent appeals from the district courts,[14] while the U.S. Supreme Court possesses discretionary authority to review cases decided by the Federal Circuit.[15]

FUNDAMENTALS OF REGULATORY EXCLUSIVITY

The U.S. government regulates the marketing of pharmaceuticals and agricultural chemicals in the interest of public health. Under this regime, the developer of a new drug—known as its "sponsor"—must demonstrate that the product is safe and effective before it can be distributed to the public.[16] This showing requires a sponsor to conduct both preclinical and clinical investigations of drugs that have not been previously tested.[17] In deciding whether to issue marketing approval or not, the FDA evaluates the test data that the sponsor submits in a so-called New Drug Application (NDA).[18]

The FDA maintains the test data incorporated into an NDA in confidence.[19] In addition, because the required test data is usually quite costly to generate, sponsors of new pharmaceuticals ordinarily do not disclose them to the public. Otherwise the sponsor's competitors could file their own NDAs using that test data, and thereby avoid the expenses of developing the information themselves.[20]

Until 1984, federal law contained no separate provisions addressing generic versions of brand-name drugs that the FDA had previously approved for marketing. The result was that a would-be generic drug manufacturer had to file its own NDA in order to market its drug. Some generic manufacturers could rely on published scientific literature demonstrating the safety and efficacy of the drug. Because these sorts of studies were not available for all drugs, however, not all generic firms could file these so-called "paper NDAs."[21] Further, at times the FDA would request additional studies to address safety and efficacy questions that arose from experience with the drug following its initial approval. The result was that some generic manufacturers were forced to prove independently that their pharmaceuticals were safe and effective, even though their products were chemically identical to those of previously approved drugs. [22]

Some commentators believed that the approval of a generic drug was a needlessly costly, redundant, and time-consuming process under this system. These observers noted that although patents on important drugs had expired, manufacturers were not moving to introduce generic equivalents for these products due to the level of resource expenditure required to obtain FDA marketing approval. As the introduction of generic equivalents often causes prices to decrease, the interest of consumers was arguably not being served through these observed costs and delays.[23]

In response to these concerns, Congress enacted the Drug Price Competition and Patent Term Restoration Act of 1984,[24] more commonly known as the Hatch-Waxman Act. This legislation created a new type of application for market approval of a generic drug. This application, termed an "Abbreviated New Drug Application" (ANDA), may be filed at the FDA.[25] An ANDA may be filed if the active ingredient of the generic drug is the bioequivalent of the approved drug. An ANDA allows a generic drug manufacturer to rely upon the safety and efficacy data of the original manufacturer. The availability of the ANDA mechanism often allows a generic manufacturer to avoid the costs and delays associated with filing a full-fledged NDA. ANDAs also allow a generic manufacturer, in many cases, to place its FDA-approved bioequivalent drug on the market as soon as any relevant patents expire.[26]

The Hatch-Waxman Act placed certain limits upon the ability of generic competitors to reference the data generated by the manufacturers of brand-name drugs. These limitations—termed regulatory exclusivities—consist of a period of time during which a competitor's ability to obtain FDA permission to sell a generic version of a previously approved brand-name drug is restricted.[27] The federal food and drug laws establish several different sorts of regulatory exclusivities relating to new chemical entities, new clinical studies, orphan drugs, pediatric studies, generic drugs, and biologics. This report will describe each of these regulatory exclusivities below.

Data Exclusivity Versus Market Exclusivity

Regulatory exclusivities are, regrettably, not subject to a standard terminology. Some commentators employ terms such as "statutory exclusivity," "data protection," and "marketing exclusivity" synonymously with the term "regulatory exclusivity."[28] This report will instead follow the approach of a second group of writers who ascribe distinct meanings to these terms.[29] Under this latter approach, "regulatory exclusivity" is an umbrella term that refers to any FDA-administered proprietary right. Regulatory exclusivities may in turn be divided into two categories: (1) those that provide data exclusivity, alternatively known as data protection, and (2) those that provide marketing exclusivity.

The distinction between data and marketing exclusivity lies in the scope of protection that each proprietary right affords. Data exclusivity protects the safety and efficacy information—often termed the "data package"—submitted by the brand-name firm from use by generic firms. As a result, a generic firm may not rely upon that data in support of its own application for FDA marketing approval for a period of years. Data exclusivity does not prevent a generic firm from submitting its own data package. In contrast, a marketing exclusivity prevents a competing firm from obtaining FDA approval whether or not it has generated its own safety and efficacy data. [30]

For many firms the distinction between a data exclusivity and marketing exclusivity may be more apparent than real. The expense of generating clinical data and other information needed to obtain marketing approval from the FDA is prohibitive for many firms.[31] The difference between data and marketing exclusivity is of greater moment to firms that can afford to generate their own data packages for submission to the FDA.

New Chemical Entity Exclusivity

The Hatch-Waxman Act established a five-year data exclusivity that is available to drugs that qualify as a new chemical entity (NCE). The purpose of this "NCE exclusivity" is to encourage the development of innovative drug products that include an entirely new active ingredient (commonly termed the "active moiety"), in contrast to "me-too" drugs that incorporate chemical variants of previously known compounds.[32] NCE exclusivity prevents a subsequent generic applicant from relying upon the data submitted by the innovative drug company during a five-year period. As a result, generic firms are precluded from relying upon this data for five years from the date of the approval of the NDA for that active moiety.[33]

A drug is judged to be an NCE if the FDA has not previously approved that drug's active ingredient.[34] During that five-year period of NCE exclusivity, the FDA may not accept a generic drug company's application to market a drug product containing the same active moiety protected under the NCE exclusivity. This prohibition holds even if these applications are directed toward a different use, dosage form, or ester or salt of the active ingredient.

As noted, NCE exclusivity acts as data exclusivity. It therefore does not preclude the FDA from accepting an application submitted by an entity that has performed all the required preclinical and clinical studies itself.[35]

The Hatch-Waxman Act allows the five-year term of NCE exclusivity to be decreased to four years under one circumstance. If the NDA holder owns patents that the generic applicant believes are invalid or not infringed, then the generic applicant is allowed to file its application one year early—upon the expiration of four, rather than five years from the date the NDA was approved.[36] The apparent purpose of this provision is to allow additional time for brand-name and generic pharmaceutical firms to put their patent affairs in order prior to generic marketing.

The practical effect of NCE exclusivity is to restrict a potential generic manufacturer from bringing a product to market for five years plus the length of the FDA review of the generic application. If, for example, the FDA requires two years to approve a particular generic application, the real-world impact of the NCE exclusivity has been seven years of protection.[37] In this respect NCE exclusivity operates differently from other forms of FDA-administered exclusivities. These exclusivities generally prevent the FDA from approving applications, rather than accepting them in the first instance.

New Clinical Study Exclusivity

In order to encourage improvements upon drugs that are already in use, the Hatch-Waxman Act also provided for a three-year new clinical study exclusivity period. New clinical study exclusivity may be awarded with respect to an NDA that contains reports of new clinical studies conducted by the sponsor that are essential to FDA approval of that application. The FDA has granted new clinical study exclusivity for such changes as new dosage forms, new indications, or for a switch from prescription to over-the-counter status for the drug.[38]

The Hatch-Waxman Act imposes four requirements that an investigation must fulfill in order to qualify for new clinical study exclusivity.[39] First, the study must be new, in that it could not have been previously used for another FDA drug approval proceeding. Second, the study must be a clinical study on humans, as compared to a preclinical or other sort of study. Third, the study must have been "conducted or sponsored" by the applicant. FDA regulations stipulate that an applicant that has provided "substantial support" for the investigation fulfills this requirement. The statement of a certified public accountant that the applicant provided 50% or more of the cost of conducting the study qualifies as substantial support, and the FDA will also entertain explanations of why the applicant should be considered to have "conducted or sponsored" the study if the applicant provided less than half of the funding for that study.[40]

Finally, the study must be "essential to the approval" of the application or supplement. The FDA has defined the term "essential to approval" as meaning "that there are no other data available that could support approval of the application." A study that provides useful background information, but is not essential to approving the change in the drug, does not provide sufficient basis for an FDA award of new clinical study exclusivity.[41]

As with NCE exclusivity, new clinical study exclusivity acts as data exclusivity.[42] It therefore does not preclude the FDA from approving a full NDA. If the sponsor of that subsequent NDA has performed all the required preclinical and clinical studies itself, the FDA may approve the NDA without regard to the new clinical trial exclusivity.

In contrast to NCE exclusivity, new clinical study exclusivity does not prevent the FDA from accepting a generic application with respect to the drug. If the new clinical study exclusivity continues to bar the issuance of marketing approval at the close of FDA review, the FDA will issue a tentative approval for the generic product that will become effective once the new clinical study exclusivity has run its course.[43]

In addition, new clinical study exclusivity only applies to the use of the product that was supported by the new clinical study. If, for example, the new studies support a new indication or dosage form of the previously approved ingredient, then the three-year exclusivity applies only to that particular use or dosage form. The FDA is not barred from approving generic drugs for other indications or dosage forms.[44]

A drug product may be subject both to NCE exclusivity and new clinical study exclusivity during the life of that product. Commonly, a new drug will initially enjoy a five-year NCE exclusivity. Later in the life of that product, the sponsor of the drug may perform additional clinical trials to qualify the drug for additional three-year exclusivities.[45]

Orphan Drug Exclusivity

In 1982, Congress enacted the Orphan Drug Act[46] in order to encourage firms to develop pharmaceuticals to treat rare diseases and conditions. Such drugs are called "orphan drugs" because firms may lack the financial incentives to sponsor products to treat small patient populations. Congressional encouragement takes a number of forms under the Orphan Drug Act, including FDA protocol assistance, tax breaks, and a grants program through which researchers may compete for grants to conduct clinical trials to support the approval of orphan drugs.[47]

The most commercially significant of all of these benefits is a seven-year term of marketing exclusivity.[48] This period commences from the date the FDA issues marketing approval on the drug. The original version of the Orphan Drug Act extended marketing approval only to drugs that were not patented. However, Congress amended the statute in 1985 to provide for regulatory exclusivity both for patented and unpatented products.[49]

Because it acts as a marketing exclusivity, orphan drug exclusivity blocks competitors from obtaining FDA approval whether or not they have generated their own data. Orphan drug regulatory exclusivity applies only to the indication for which the drug is approved, however. As a result, the FDA could approve a second application of the same drug for a different use. The FDA cannot approve the same drug made by another manufacturer for the same use, however, unless the original sponsor approves or the original sponsor is unable to provide sufficient quantities of the drug to the market.[50]

As originally enacted, the Orphan Drug Act defined an orphan drug as one for which there was no "reasonable expectation that the cost of developing ... will be recovered from sales in the United States of such drug."[51] In 1984, Congress changed the definition to its present form.[52] Currently, in order to qualify for orphan drug status, the drug must treat a rare disease or condition (1) affecting less than 200,000 people in the United States, or (2) affecting more than 200,000 people in the United States, but for which there is no reasonable expectation that the sales of the drug would recover the costs.[53] As can be appreciated, the effect of this change was to allow drug sponsors to avoid making a showing of unprofitability if the target population consisted of less than 200,000 persons.

The original version of the Orphan Drug Act allowed a sponsor to request orphan drug status at any time prior to FDA marketing approval. Congress amended the statute in 1988, however, to require that the sponsor make this designation request prior to the submission of an application for marketing approval.[54]

Biologics Exclusivity

The Biologics Price Competition and Innovation Act of 2009 (BPCIA), which was enacted as Title VII of the Patient Protection and Affordable Care Act, introduced new regulatory exclusivities for a category of biologically derived preparations known as "biologics." Biologics consist of such products as vaccines, antitoxins, blood components, and therapeutic serums.[55] For the most part, the FDA regulates biologics under Section 351 of the Public Health Service Act,[56] as compared to the Federal Food, Drug, and Cosmetic Act[57] which applies to small-molecule, traditional pharmaceuticals.

The BPCIA established two periods of regulatory exclusivity applicable to brand-name biologics, one with a duration of 4 years and the other with a duration of 12 years. The BPCIA specifically provides:

> (7) EXCLUSIVITY FOR REFERENCE PRODUCT.—
>
> (A) EFFECTIVE DATE OF BIOSIMILAR APPLICATION APPROVAL.—Approval of an application under this subsection may not be made effective by the Secretary until the date that is 12 years after the date on which the reference product was first licensed under subsection (a).
>
> '(B) FILING PERIOD.—An application under this subsection may not be submitted to the Secretary until the date that is 4 years after the date on which the reference product was first licensed under subsection (a).[58]

Some discussion has occurred about whether the 12-year regulatory exclusivity period identified in the statute operates as a data or marketing exclusivity. In the FDA's public hearing notice, the agency referred to a "12-year period of marketing exclusivity."[59] Several Members of Congress drafted letters to the FDA explaining that the 12-year period instead acted as a data exclusivity. One letter explained:

> The Act does not provide market exclusivity for innovator products. It provides data exclusivity, which prohibits FDA from allowing another manufacturer of a highly similar biologic to rely on the Agency's prior finding of safety, purity and potency for the innovator product for a limited period of time. It does not prohibit or prevent another manufacturer from developing its own data to justify FDA approval of a full biologics license application rather than an abbreviated application that relies on the prior approval of a reference product.[60]

Similarly, other Members of Congress explained that the 12-year regulatory exclusivity acts as data exclusivity that "only protects the FDA from allowing another manufacturer to rely on the data of an innovator to support another product. Importantly, it does not prohibit or prevent another manufacturer from developing its own data to justify FDA approval of a similar of competitive product."[61]

A third letter from Members of Congress stated their belief that "the statute is clear that the FDA can begin reviewing biogeneric applications during the 12 year exclusivity period."[62] The FDA subsequently issued a draft guidance document that appeared to align the agency's view with that of the congressional correspondents.[63]

Pediatric Exclusivity

Brand-name firms may qualify for a six-month pediatric exclusivity upon the completion of studies on the effects of a drug upon children.[64] This six-month period begins on the date that the existing patent or data exclusivity protection on the innovator drug would otherwise expire. Pediatric exclusivity extends to any drug product with the same active ingredient (also known as the drug's "active moiety").

The purpose of the pediatric regulatory exclusivity is to improve the availability of appropriate pediatric labeling on drug products.[65]

Congress first established pediatric regulatory exclusivities with the Food and Drug Administration Modernization Act of 1997 (FDAMA).[66] Although the FDAMA included a sunset provision, Congress subsequently reauthorized these provisions.[67]

In the 112th Congress, the Food and Drug Administration Safety and Innovation Act, P.L. 112-144, made the pediatric exclusivity permanent.[68]

In establishing pediatric exclusivity, Congress responded to concerns that many FDA-approved drugs had not yet been clinically tested upon children. Investigations upon a pediatric population tends to raise a number of complexities, including issues of informed consent, the changes that occur in children as they grow, and the inability of children to describe accurately the effect of a medication.

As a result, most drugs are tested solely upon adults. By establishing a pediatric regulatory exclusivity, Congress hoped to encourage additional pediatric testing, which in turn could allow medications to be labeled for use by children.[69]

Pursuant to its statutory authority, the FDA issues written requests to NDA applicants and holders to perform pediatric studies with respect to the drug.

An FDA written request contains such information as the indications and the number of patients to be studied, the labeling that may result from such studies, the format of the report to be submitted to the FDA, and the timeframe for completing the studies. Response to this written request is wholly voluntary.

If the innovative drug company submits a report to the satisfaction of the FDA, however, then it will be awarded the six-month pediatric regulatory exclusivity.[70]

Notably, the food and drug laws do not condition pediatric exclusivity upon the success of the study. The six-month regulatory exclusivity period may be obtained whether or not the study successfully demonstrates safety and effectiveness in children. Thus, the pediatric exclusivity is intended to create incentives for drug sponsors to conduct research and submit their results to the FDA.[71]

The effect of a pediatric exclusivity is to extend the approved manufacturer's existing regulatory exclusivity or patent protection for an additional six months. If the pediatric exclusivity applied to an orphan drug, for example, the result would be seven years and six months of marketing exclusivity; if applied to an NCE exclusivity, the drug's sponsor would obtain five years and six months of data protection.

If applied to a patent, that pediatric exclusivity does not actually extend the term of a patent; rather, it is a regulatory exclusivity administered by the FDA.[72]

Qualified Infectious Disease Products

Congressional concern over the spread of antibiotic-resistant "superbugs" recently led to the enactment of the Generating Antibiotic Incentives Now (GAIN) Act, enacted as Title VIII of the FDA Safety and Innovation Act, P.L. 112-144. [73] That statute allows the FDA to designate a drug as a "qualified infectious disease product" (QIDP) if it consists of an antibacterial or antifungal drug intended to treat serious or life-threatening infections.[74] The GAIN Act stipulates that QIDPs include drugs that address drug-resistant tuberculosis, gram negative bacteria, and Staphylococcus aureus.[75]

Along with other measures intended to provide pharmaceutical and biotechnology companies with incentives to develop innovative antibiotics,[76] the GAIN Act adds five years to the term of the new chemical entity, new clinical study, and orphan exclusivities for any QIDP.[77] The statute stipulates that the five-year QIDP extension is cumulative with the pediatric exclusivity.[78] As a result, a QIDP that qualified as a new chemical entity, and was also awarded a pediatric exclusivity, would be entitled to a data exclusivity period of ten years and six months.

Generic and Follow-On Exclusivity

Most of the regulatory exclusivities operate in favor of brand-name firms. However, federal law also establishes regulatory exclusivities designed to encourage generic and follow-on firms to market their products. The Hatch-Waxman Act allows generic firms to obtain a 180-day period of "generic exclusivity" if they are the first to file an ANDA challenging a brand-name firm's patents.[79] Generally speaking, this regulatory exclusivity precludes the FDA from approving another ANDA for the same product for the 180-day period.[80]

In addition, the Biologics Price Competition and Innovation Act of 2009 establishes a regulatory exclusivity that operates in favor of manufacturers of follow-on biologics. Under the BPCIA, the first follow-on product deemed to be interchangeable with the brand-name product is entitled to a period of exclusivity before the FDA will make a determination of interchangeability for a competing product. Follow-on exclusivity ends at the earlier of one year after first commercial marketing, 18 months after a final court decision in a patent infringement action against the applicant or dismissal of such an action,

42 months after approval if the applicant has been sued and the litigation is still ongoing, or 18 months after approval if the applicant has not been sued.[81]

Innovation Policy Issues

The Term of Regulatory Exclusivities

The Obama Administration has proposed a reduction in the regulatory exclusivity offered to brand-name biologic drugs to seven years, down from the 12 years incorporated in the Biologics Price Competition and Innovation Act of 2009. The Obama Administration's Fiscal Year 2013 Budget asserted that the shorter periods of data exclusivity will "encourage faster development of generic biologics while retaining appropriate incentives for research and development for the innovation of breakthrough products." [82] This change would purportedly result in $4 billion in savings over 10 years to federal health programs including Medicare and Medicaid. This proposal has yet to be enacted.

Regulatory Exclusivity for Colchicine

Controversy surrounded the award of regulatory exclusivities to colchicine, an ancient remedy for gout that had been marketed for decades in the United States without FDA approval.[83] In 2006, the FDA launched an Unapproved Drugs Initiative to encourage manufacturers of old drugs that were sold prior to current premarket approval requirements to test the drugs for safety and efficacy and to seek formal agency approval.[84] The FDA had previously approved two combination products including colchicine as one of multiple ingredients, but had never approved a single-ingredient colchicine product.[85]

In response to the FDA request, one firm submitted NDAs for the use of colchicine to treat familial Mediterranean fever and acute gout flares. The FDA approved both applications and awarded seven years of orphan drug exclusivity for the use of colchicine to treat familial Mediterranean fever and three years of new clinical study exclusivity for the treatment of acute gout flares. The FDA subsequently announced its intention to take enforcement action against unapproved single-ingredient colchicine products.[86] With other suppliers removed from the market, the new sole provider reportedly increased the price of its colchicine product, Colcrys®, from $0.09 to $4.85 per tablet.[87]

As a practical matter, regulatory exclusivities ordinarily apply only to products that are coming to the market for the first time. The colchicine incident nonetheless illustratcs that, unlike patent protection, regulatory exclusivities may be awarded to products that are not necessarily new or innovative. This case also illustrates the costs that regulatory exclusivities may impose upon patients and payors for drugs that might have been sold far more cheaply in a competitive market.

The MODDERN Cures Act

As a historical matter, patents have long served as a primary incentive for health care innovation in the United States. Regulatory exclusivities are a relatively more recent form of intellectual property right, first coming into being in the 1980s with the Orphan Drug and Hatch-Waxman Acts. Because regulatory exclusivities have traditionally offered shorter periods of protection than the 20-year patent term, patents are often viewed as the principal R&D incentive mechanism for the pharmaceutical and biotechnology sectors. However, legislation has been introduced in the 112th Congress that would establish a distinct framework of innovation incentives that emphasizes regulatory exclusivity over patents.

Under H.R. 3497, the proposed Modernizing Our Drug & Diagnostics Evaluation and Regulatory Network Cures Act (MODDERN Cures Act), a drug sponsor could submit a request to FDA for "dormant therapy" designation for a therapy that fulfills an "unmet medical need" and that has "prospectively insufficient patent protection."[88] The request must include a list of patents covering the therapy and a conditional waiver of the right to enforce those patents after the termination of regulatory exclusivity. If the FDA agrees that the indication for which approval is sought addresses an unmet medical need, it will grant the dormant therapy designation and the patent waiver will become effective. The sponsor then obtains 15 years of marketing exclusivity. All of the identified patents are given an extended term of up to 15 years after the product is approved, but pursuant to the patent waiver, the sponsor of the drug disclaims any patent term after the 15-year exclusivity period.[89]

The MODDERN Cures Act confronts policy makers with a debate previously conducted by legal academics over the relative role of patents and regulatory exclusivities in promoting pharmaceutical and biotechnology R&D.

Regulatory exclusivity arguably provides a better temporal fit with the life cycle of a pharmaceutical or biologic product than does a patent. Regulatory exclusivity periods typically do not begin until a drug is on the market, while much or all of a patent term may run before the FDA grants marketing approval.[90] The scope of regulatory exclusivities may also correspond more closely to relevant product markets than do patents. Regulatory exclusivity tracks the terms of FDA product approvals, while patent claims, drafted to distinguish an invention from the prior art, may not correspond as closely to any actual commercial product.[91]

In addition, patents provide not so much the right to exclude as the right to sue to exclude.[92] Generic firms frequently make successful arguments that the brand-name firm's patents are invalid or not infringed. In contrast, regulatory exclusivity keeps competitors off the market without the need for patent owners to bring expensive and uncertain infringement lawsuits.

On the other hand, regulatory exclusivities arguably possess disadvantages in comparison to patents. For example, the U.S. Supreme Court recently explained that "the results of ordinary innovation are not the subject of exclusive rights under the patent laws. Were it otherwise patents might stifle, rather than promote, the progress of useful arts."[93] Yet as suggested by the colchicine incident, regulatory exclusivities are available for old products based upon the completion of routine clinical trials that would not qualify for additional patent rights. Denying patent rights to "ordinary innovation" in order to promote progress seems inconsistent with granting analogous protection via regulatory exclusivity in the context of drug testing.

Regulatory exclusivities may also place public health officials in the potentially uncomfortable position of denying patients access to safe and effective generic substitutes for unpatented medications. They require the FDA to devote considerable time and effort towards drafting regulations, issuing guidance documents, and adjudicating disputes involving multiple regulatory exclusivity regimes.[94] These resources might be more effectively spent in pursuit of the agency's core mission of protecting public health.

International Issues

The agreements comprising the World Trade Organization (WTO) impose certain requirements with respect to both patents and regulatory exclusivities. The WTO Agreement on Trade-Related Aspects of Intellectual Property (TRIPS Agreement) requires signatories to provide patent protection "without discrimination as to the place of invention, the field of technology and whether products are imported or locally produced."[95] This provision in part required WTO member states to eliminate provisions in their national laws that disallowed patents on pharmaceutical products. But the TRIPS Agreement apparently prohibits discrimination in favor of pharmaceutical patents as well as against them.

The TRIPS Agreement also requires each WTO member state to establish protections for pharmaceutical test data under certain conditions. Article 39.3 of the TRIPS Agreement specifically provides:

> Members, when requiring as a condition of approving the marketing of pharmaceutical or of agricultural chemical products which utilize new chemical entities, the submission of undisclosed test or other data, the origination of which involves a considerable effort, shall protect such data against unfair commercial use. In addition, Members shall protect such data against disclosure, except where necessary to protect the public, or unless steps are taken to ensure that the data are protected against unfair commercial use.

Some commentators have observed that Article 39.3 establishes broad parameters using vague language. In particular, terms such as "new chemical entities," "considerable effort," and "unfair commercial use" receive no further definition within the TRIPS Agreement. As a result, some debate has occurred over the precise nature of the obligations Article 39.3 imposes upon WTO member states.[96]

Perhaps given the uncertainties with respect to Article 39.3 of the TRIPS Agreement, the United States has entered into certain Free Trade Agreements (FTAs) that require signatories to provide five years of regulatory exclusivity for pharmaceuticals that utilize new chemical entities. For example, Article 15.10:1(a) of the Dominican Republic-Central America-United States FTA provides:

> If a Party requires, as a condition of approving the marketing of a new pharmaceutical or agricultural chemical product, the submission of undisclosed data concerning safety or efficacy, the Party shall not permit third persons, without the consent of the person who provided the information, to market a product on the basis of (1) the information, or (2) the approval granted to the person who submitted the information for at least five years for pharmaceutical products and ten years for agricultural chemical products from the date of approval in the Party.

The term "new product" is generally defined as "one that does not contain a chemical entity that has been previously approved in the territory of the Party."[97]

More recently, the United States has entered into negotiations with respect to the Trans-Pacific Partnership (TPP), a multilateral free trade agreement that aims to liberalize trade within the Asia-Pacific region. The TPP reportedly calls for its signatories to adopt a period of exclusivity for biologics. Some Members of Congress have encouraged U.S. negotiators to incorporate a 12-year period of exclusivity that would align the TPP with the Biologics Price Competition and Innovation Act of 2009.[98] However, other Members of Congress have expressed concern over the impact of regulatory exclusivity provisions in the TPP on healthcare in developing countries.[99]

CONCLUSION

In combination, patents and regulatory exclusivities provide the fundamental framework of intellectual property incentives for pharmaceutical innovation in the United States. Due to the TRIPS Agreement's obligation of technological neutrality with respect to the patent system, regulatory exclusivities provide Congress with a more adaptable option for stimulating specific sorts of hoped-for private activity than do patents. As such, regulatory exclusivities have been, and likely will continue to be, the most widely used option for encouraging the development of discrete classes of products regulated by the FDA.

The potential for expanded use of regulatory exclusivities in turn raises a number of innovation policy issues. In the United States, regulatory exclusivities are viewed primarily as supplementing patent protection, in that they provide more limited protections for inventions that do not meet Patent Act requirements, or effectively delay the onset of patent litigation for inventions that do. Expanding the availability of regulatory exclusivities, in addition to lengthening their term, increases the possibility that regulatory exclusivities will trump patents as the primary form of intellectual property protection for certain FDA-regulated products.

The decision to supplant the primacy of the current regime of USPTO-procured and judicially enforced patent rights with a system of automatic, FDA-administered regulatory exclusivities presents a number of trade-offs that policy makers may wish to consider. Among them are the impact of the contemplated exclusivity periods upon incentives for pharmaceutical innovation; the cost and availability of medications to consumers; the desirability of individualized determinations about the technical merits of the pharmaceutical invention; the expense and uncertainty of patent enforcement proceedings; and whether the USPTO or FDA is the better institution for awarding proprietary rights to pharmaceutical innovators.

International harmonization provides another significant issue with respect to regulatory exclusivities. While some observers have expressed concerns over the use of free trade agreements to encourage trading partners to establish longer regulatory exclusivity periods, others believe that doing so lies in the best interest of the United States. Future dialogue may concern setting global regulatory exclusivity standards in view of national goals and priorities.

End Notes

[1] P.L. 112-144 at §801.
[2] See Yaniv Heled, "Patents vs. Statutory Exclusivities in Biological Pharmaceuticals—Do We Really Need Both?," 18 Michigan Telecommunications and Technology Law Review (2012), 419.
[3] See Benjamin N. Roin, "Unpatentable Drugs and the Standards of Patentability," 87 Texas Law Review (2009), 503.
[4] See Jerome H. Reichman, "Rethinking the Role of Clinical Trial Data in International Intellectual Property Law: The Case for a Public Goods Approach," 13 Marquette Intellectual Property Law Review (2009), 1.
[5] 35 U.S.C. §111.
[6] 35 U.S.C. §112.
[7] 35 U.S.C. §111.
[8] Ibid.
[9] 35 U.S.C. §102.
[10] 35 U.S.C. §103.
[11] 35 U.S.C. §271.
[12] 35 U.S.C. §154(a).
[13] 28 U.S.C. §1339(a).
[14] 28 U.S.C. §1295(a)(1).
[15] 28 U.S.C. §1254(1).
[16] 21 U.S.C. §355.
[17] Development and Approval Process (Drugs), Food and Drug Administration, http://www.fda.gov/Drugs/DevelopmentApprovalProcess/default.htm.
[18] 21 C.F.R. §314.50.
[19] 21 C.F.R. §20.61.
[20] See Mustafa Ünlü, "It Is Time: Why the FDA Should Start Disclosing Drug Trial Data," 16 Michigan Telecommunications and Technology Law Review (2010), 511.
[21] See Colleen Kelly, "The Balance Between Innovation and Competition: The Hatch-Waxman Act, the 2003 Amendments, and Beyond," 66 Food & Drug Law Journal (2011), 417.

[22] See D. Christopher Ohly and Sailesh K. Patel, "The Hatch-Waxman Act: Prescriptions for Innovative and Inexpensive Medicines," 19 University of Baltimore Intellectual Property Law Journal (2011), 107.

[23] See Linda P. Nussbaum & John D. Radice, "Where Do We Go Now? The Hatch-Waxman Act Twenty-Five Years Later: Successes, Failures, and Prescriptions for the Future," 41 Rutgers Law Journal (2009), 229.

[24] P.L. 84-417, 98 Stat. 1585 (1984).

[25] 21 U.S.C. §355(j)(1).

[26] See Martin S. Masar III, "Effects of the Federal Circuit Judges on Hatch-Waxman Litigation," 19 DePaul Journal of Art, Technology & Intellectual Property Law (2009), 315.

[27] See Brian F. McMahon, "The Biologics Price Competition and Innovation Act of 2009: Legislative Imprudence, Patent Devaluation, and the False Start of a Multi-Billion Dollar Industry," 100 Kentucky Law Review (2011-12), 635.

[28] See John R. Thomas, Pharmaceutical Patent Law (Bureau of National Affairs, 2d ed. 2010) (noting these terminological distinctions).

[29] See, e.g., Maxwell R. Morgan, "Regulation of Innovation Under Follow-On Biologics Legislation: FDA Exclusivity as an Efficient Incentive Mechanism," 11 Columbia Science and Technology Law Review (2010), 93.

[30] See McMahon, supra.

[31] See Rebecca S. Eisenberg, "The Role of the FDA in Innovation Policy," 13 Michigan Telecommunications and Technology Law Review (2007), 345.

[32] See Robert Alan Hess, "Excavating Treasure from the Amber of the Prior Art; Why the Public Benefit Doctrine Is Ill-Suited to the Pharmaceutical Sciences," 66 Food & Drug Law Journal (2011), 105.

[33] 21 U.S.C. §355(j)(5)(F)(ii).

[34] 21 C.F.R. §314.108(a).

[35] See Timothy A. Cook, "Pharmaceutical Patent Litigation Settlements: Balancing Patient & Antirust Policy Through Institutional Choice," 17 Michigan Telecommunications and Technology Law Review (2011), 417.

[36] See C. Scott Hemphill & Mark A. Lemley, "Earning Exclusivity: Generic Drug Incentives and the Hatch-Waxman Act," 77 Antitrust Law Journal (2011), 947.

[37] See Joyce Wing Yan Tam, "Biologics Revolution: The Intersection of Biotechnology, Patent Law, and Pharmaceutical Regulation," 98 Georgetown Law Journal (2010), 535.

[38] See Elizabeth H. Dickinson, "FDA's Role in Making Exclusivity Determinations," 54 Food and Drug Law Journal (1999), 195.

[39] 21 U.S.C. §355(j)(5)(F)(iii)-(iv).

[40] 21 C.F.R. §314.108(a).

[41] Ibid.

[42] See Anna B. Laakmann, "Collapsing the Distinction Between Experimentation and Treatment in the Regulation of New Drugs," 62 Alabama Law Review (2011), 305.

[43] See Dickinson, supra.

[44] See Rebecca S. Eisenberg, "The Problem of New Uses," 5 Yale Journal of Health Policy, Law and Ethics (2005), 717.

[45] See Brook K. Baker, "Ending Drug Registration Apartheid: Taming Data Exclusivity and Patent/Registration Linkage," 34 American Journal of Law and Medicine (2008), 303.

[46] P.L. 97-414, 96 Stat. 2049 (1982).

[47] See David Duffield Rohde, "The Orphan Drug Act: An Engine of Innovation? At What Cost?," 55 Food and Drug Law Journal (2000), 125.

[48] 21 U.S.C. §360cc.
[49] Orphan Drug Amendments of 1985, P.L. 99-91.
[50] 21 U.S.C. §360cc(b).
[51] P.L. 97-414, §526(a)(2), 96 Stat. 2049 (1982).
[52] Health Promotion and Disease Prevention Amendments of 1984, P.L. 98-551, 98 Stat. 2815 (1984).
[53] 21 U.S.C. §360bb(a)(2).
[54] Orphan Drug Amendments of 1988, P.L. 100-290, 102 Stat. 90 (1988).
[55] 42 U.S.C. §262(i).
[56] This provision has been codified as 42 U.S.C. §262.
[57] P.L. 98-417, 98 Stat. 1585.
[58] 42 U.S.C. §262(k)(7).
[59] Dept. Health & Human Servs., FDA, "Approval Pathway for Biosimilar and Interchangeable Biological Products; Public Hearing; Request for Comments," 75 Federal Register (Oct. 5, 2010), 61497.
[60] Letter of January 7, 2011, from Senator Michael Enzi et al., to Dr. Margaret Hamburg, Commissioner, FDA (available at http://www.hpm.com/pdf/1-7-11%20Senate%20Biologics%20letter%20to%20FDA.pdf) (signed by Senators Enzi, Hagan, Hatch, and Kerry).
[61] See Letter of December 21, 2010, from Representative Anna G. Eshoo et al., to FDA (available at http://patentdocs.typepad.com/files/letter-to-fda.pdf)(signed by Representatives Barton, Eshoo, and Inslee).
[62] See Letter of January 24, 2011, from Senator Sherrod Brown et al., to Dr. Margaret Hamburg, Commissioner, FDA (available at http://patentdocs.typepad.com/files/senator-letters-exclusivity.pdf) (signed by Senators Brown, Harkin, McCain, and Schumer).
[63] FDA, Guidance for Industry, Biosimilars: Questions and Answers Regarding Implementation of the Biologics Price Competition and Innovation Act of 2009 (Feb. 2012), 3.
[64] 21 U.S.C. §355a.
[65] See Michael J. Malinowski & Grant G. Gautreaux, "Drug Development—Stuck in a State of Puberty?: Regulatory Reform of Human Clinical Research to Raise Responsiveness to the Reality of Human Variability," 56 St. Louis University Law Journal (2012), 363.
[66] P.L. 105-115, 111 Stat. 2296, at §11 (1997).
[67] See Thomas, supra, at 461.
[68] P.L. 112-144 at §501.
[69] See Scott Tillett, "Off-Label Prescribing of SSRIs to Children: Should Pediatric Testing Be Required, or Are There Other Means to a Safer End for Children?," 19 Southern California Review of Law & Social Justice (2010), 447.
[70] See Barbara A. Noah, "Just a Spoonful of Sugar: Drug Safety for Pediatric Populations," 37 Journal of Law, Medicine and Ethics 280 (2009).
[71] See Leslie Kushner, "Incentivizing Postmarketing Pharmaceutical Product Safety Testing with Extension of Exclusivity Periods," 19 Fordham Intellectual Property, Media and Entertainment Law Journal (2009), 519.
[72] Ibid.
[73] P.L. 112-144, §801 (introducing 21 U.S.C. §505E).
[74] 21 U.S.C. §505E(g).
[75] 21 U.S.C. §505E(f).
[76] See "Antibiotics Resistance Rising; Can New Drugs Keep Pace?", BioWorld Insight (September 17, 2012).

[77] 21 U.S.C. §505E(a).
[78] 21 U.S.C. §505E(b).
[79] 21 U.S.C. §355(j)(B)(iv).
[80] See, e.g., David E. Korn et al., "A New History and Discussion of 180-Day Exclusivity," 64 Food and Drug Law Journal (2009), 335.
[81] 42 U.S.C. §262(k)(6).
[82] Office of Management and Budget, Fiscal Year 2013 Budget of the U.S. Government, at 37.
[83] Aaron S. Kesselheim & Daniel H. Solomon, "Incentives for Drug Development—The Curious Case of Colchicine," 362 New England Journal of Medicine (2010), 2045.
[84] FDA, Guidance for FDA Staff and Industry: Marketed Unapproved Drugs: Compliance Policy Guide (2011), available at http://www.fda.gov/downloads/Drugs/ Guidance ComplianceRegulatoryInformation/Guidances/ ucm070290.pdf.
[85] FDA, Letter to Gary L. Veron, Esq. from Janet Woodcock, Director, Center for Drug Evaluation and Research (May 25, 2011), available at http://www.regulations.gov /#!documentDetail;D=FDA-2010-P-0614-0072.
[86] FDA, "Single-Ingredient Oral Colchicine Products; Enforcement Action Dates," 75 Federal Register (October 1, 2010), 60768.
[87] Kesselheim & Solomon, supra.
[88] H.R. 3497, §201.
[89] Ibid. at §202.
[90] Eisenberg (2007), supra.
[91] Ibid.
[92] Mark A. Lemley & Carl Shapiro, "Probabilistic Patents," Journal of Economic Perspectives (Spring 2005), 75.
[93] KSR International Co. v. Teleflex Inc., 550 U.S. 398, 427 (2007).
[94] Eisenberg (2007), supra.
[95] Agreement on Trade-Related Aspects of Intellectual Property Rights, April 15, 1994, Annex 1C, 33 I.L.M. 1197 (1994), Art. 27.
[96] See Trudo Lemmens & Candice Telfer, "Access to Information and the Right to Health: The Human Rights Case for Clinical Trials Transparency," 38 American Journal of Law & Medicine (2012), 63.
[97] Dominican Republic-Central America-United States Free Trade Agreement, January 1, 2006, 119 Stat. 462, at Chapter 15, footnote 15.
[98] Letter from Senators Patty Murray and Maria Cantwell to President Barack Obama (July 12, 2012) (available at http://www.hpm.com/pdf/blog/WA%20TPP%20letter.pdf).
[99] Letter from Rep. Jan Schakowksy et al., to Ambassador Ron Kirk, Office of the U.S. Trade Representative (August 2, 2011) (available at http://infojustice.org/wp-content/ uploads/2011/08/Ten-Representatives-on-TPP-08022011.pdf).

In: Pharmaceutical Patents
Editor: Florian Aerts

ISBN: 978-1-62618-758-0

Chapter 3

Patent Infringement and Experimental Use under the Hatch-Waxman Act: Current Issues*

John R. Thomas

Summary

Concerns over the availability of affordable health care have focused national attention upon patents and other intellectual property rights awarded to pharmaceutical firms. Legislation that was introduced before, but not enacted by, the 112th Congress proposed amendments to the Hatch-Waxman Act, legislation dating from 1984 that governs intellectual property rights in pharmaceuticals and other regulated products. Recent rulings from the federal judiciary regarding the Hatch-Waxman Act may be pertinent to future congressional consideration of that statute. Both the judicial holdings, as well as possible legislative changes to the Hatch-Waxman Act, potentially affect the availability of both brand-name and generic drugs in the United States.

The Hatch-Waxman Act includes two core provisions that impact the enforcement of patent rights by brand-name firms against generic

* This is an edited, reformatted and augmented version of a Congressional Research Service publication, CRS Report for Congress R42354, from www.crs.gov, prepared for Members and Committees of Congress, dated January 17, 2013.

pharmaceutical companies. 35 U.S.C. §271(e)(1) creates a statutory "safe harbor" that exempts firms from claims of patent infringement based on clinical trials and other acts reasonably related to seeking marketing approval from the Food and Drug Administration (FDA). The explicit wording of that statute does not preclude activities that occur after the receipt of FDA marketing approval from the "safe harbor." Two recent opinions from the U.S. Court of Appeals for the Federal Circuit are arguably in tension over whether post-approval acts are exempted from infringement, however.

A second provision, 35 U.S.C. §271(e)(2), allows a brand-name drug company to enforce its patents against a potential generic competitor at such time that the generic firm files an application—a so-called Abbreviated New Drug Application (ANDA)—with the FDA seeking marketing approval. Although courts have stated that this litigation may only be based upon patents identified to the FDA and listed in the so-called "Orange Book," the express wording of the statute does not appear to impose this requirement. This issue has yet to be conclusively resolved in the courts.

Should Congress conclude that the current situation with respect to 35 U.S.C. §271(e) is satisfactory, no action need be taken. If Congress wishes to intervene, however, then some options present themselves. Congress could stipulate whether 35 U.S.C. §271(e)(1) applies to acts that occur following the award of FDA marketing approval or not. Congress could also explicitly state whether 35 U.S.C. §271(e)(2) establishes a cause of action for infringement of patents that have not been listed in the Orange Book.

BACKGROUND

The high cost and availability of health care in the United States have focused attention upon patents and other intellectual property rights available to pharmaceutical firms. Of particular moment to this discussion is the Hatch-Waxman Act, legislation that governs intellectual property rights with respect to pharmaceuticals and other regulated products. More formally known as the Drug Price Competition and Patent Term Restoration Act of 1984,[1] this legislation is widely regarding as having a strong impact upon the availability of both brand-name and generic pharmaceuticals in the United States.[2]

The Hatch-Waxman Act includes two core provisions addressing the enforcement of pharmaceutical patents. The first of those, 35 U.S.C. §271(e)(1), creates a statutory "safe harbor" that exempts firms from claims of patent infringement based on clinical trials and other acts reasonably related to seeking marketing approval from the Food and Drug Administration (FDA).[3] A second provision, 35 U.S.C. §271(e)(2), allows a brand-name drug company to enforce its patents against a potential generic competitor at such time that the generic firm files an application—a so-called Abbreviated New Drug Application (ANDA)—with thc FDA seeking marketing approval. In support of the brand-name firm's intellectual property rights, the FDA publishes information pertaining to patents that the brand-name firm identifies to the agency.[4] If the generic firm does not agree to wait until these patents expire before marketing its product, then the brand-name firm may commence patent infringement litigation immediately.[5]

Recent judicial developments have involved both provisions. Two recent judgments from the U.S. Court of Appeals for the Federal Circuit are arguably in tension as to whether the statutory safe harbor is limited to activities performed prior to the award of FDA approval.[6] Because 35 U.S.C. §271(e)(1) does not expressly restrict its scope to premarketing approval efforts,[7] these holdings have been the subject of considerable discussion. As well, brand-name firms have attempted to assert patents against generic firms that they have not explicitly identified to the FDA. Although the Supreme Court has suggested that such identification is a predicate for litigation,[8] 35 U.S.C. §271(e)(2) does not expressly state as much.[9] The courts have yet to rule definitively on this point.

This report will discuss current issues with respect to the patent infringement provisions of the Hatch-Waxman Act. The report begins by laying out the basics of the Hatch-Waxman patent dispute resolution system. It then describes the recent holdings of the Court of Appeals for the Federal Circuit in *Classen Immunotherapies LLC v. Biogen Idec*[10] and *Momenta Pharmaceuticals, Inc. v. Amphastar Pharmaceuticals, Inc.*,[11] concerning the applicability of the statutory safe harbor to activities that occur subsequent to FDA approval. Next, the report considers judicial developments regarding the patent infringement provision of the Hatch-Waxman Act. This report closes with a review of pertinent legislative issues.

INTRODUCTION TO THE HATCH-WAXMAN ACT

The Hatch-Waxman Act brings together two previously distinct legal regimes, the patent law and the food and drug law. Under the latter regime, the sponsor of a new drug must demonstrate that the product is safe and effective in order to obtain FDA approval. This showing typically requires the drug's sponsor to conduct both preclinical and clinical investigations.[12] In deciding whether to issue marketing approval or not, the FDA evaluates the test data that the sponsor submits in a so-called New Drug Application (NDA).

Prior to the enactment of the Hatch-Waxman Act, the federal food and drug law contained no separate provisions addressing marketing approval for generic versions of drugs that had previously been approved by the FDA.[13] The result was that a would-be generic drug manufacturer had to file its own NDA in order to sell its product.[14] Some generic manufacturers could rely on published scientific literature demonstrating the safety and efficacy of the drug by submitting a so-called paper NDA. Because these sorts of studies were not available for all drugs, however, not all generic firms could file a so-called paper NDA.[15] Further, at times the FDA requested additional studies to address safety and efficacy questions that arose from experience with the drug following its initial approval.[16] Consequently, some generic manufacturers were forced to prove once more that a particular drug was safe and effective, even though their products were chemically identical to those of previously approved pharmaceuticals.

Some commentators believed that the approval of a generic drug was a needlessly costly, duplicative, and time-consuming process.[17] These observers noted that although patents on important drugs had expired, manufacturers were not moving to introduce generic equivalents for these products due to the level of resource expenditure required to obtain FDA marketing approval.[18]

In response to these concerns, Congress enacted the Hatch-Waxman Act, a statute that has been described as a "complex and multifaceted compromise between innovative and generic pharmaceutical companies."[19] Its provisions include a new statutory pathway, the Abbreviated New Drug Application or ANDA, which expedites the marketing approval process for generic drugs. An ANDA allows a generic applicant to obtain marketing approval by demonstrating that the proposed product is bioequivalent to an approved pioneer drug. Unlike brand-name firms, generic drug companies are not required to undertake costly and time-consuming clinical trials in order to demonstrate the safety and effectiveness of their products.

Patent Infringement Dispute Resolution

When drafting the Hatch-Waxman Act, Congress recognized that brand-name pharmaceutical firms may be the proprietors of one or more patents directed towards their products. These patents might be infringed by a product described by a generic firm's ANDA in the event that product is approved by the FDA and sold in the marketplace. The Hatch-Waxman Act therefore established special procedures for resolving patent disputes in connection with applications for marketing generic drugs. Reflecting its compromise nature, the legislation both provides an exemption for patent infringement (for FDA regulatory compliance activities) and creates a new infringing act (the filing of certain ANDAs by generic firms).

First, the Hatch-Waxman Act established a statutory research exemption to patent infringement. 35 U.S.C. §271(e)(1) applies "solely to uses reasonably related to the development and submission of information under a Federal law which regulates the manufacture, use, or sale of drugs or veterinary biological products." The Supreme Court has observed that although "the contours of this provision are not exact in every respect, the statutory text makes clear that it provides a wide berth for the use of patented drugs in activities related to the federal regulatory process."[20] This statutory "safe harbor" most commonly operates in favor of generic firms who wish to perform activities, including bioequivalence studies, prior to filing their ANDAs.

The Hatch-Waxman also establishes a new cause of action for infringement. 35 U.S.C. §271(e)(2) states that each NDA applicant "shall file" a list of patents that the applicant believes would be infringed if a generic drug were marketed prior to the expiration of these patents.[21] The FDA then lists these patents in a publication titled *Approved Drug Products with Therapeutic Equivalence Evaluations*, which is more commonly known as the "Orange Book."[22] Would-be manufacturers of generic drugs must then engage in a specialized certification procedure with respect to Orange Book-listed patents. An ANDA applicant must state its views with respect to each Orange Book-listed patent associated with the drug it seeks to market. Four possibilities exist:

1) that the brand-name firm has not filed any patent information with respect to that drug;
2) that the patent has already expired;
3) that the generic company agrees not to market until the date on which the patent will expire; or
4) that the patent is invalid or will not be infringed by the manufacture, use or sale of the drug for which the ANDA is submitted.[23]

These certifications are respectively termed paragraph I, II, III, and IV certifications.[24] An ANDA application certified under paragraphs I or II is approved immediately after meeting all applicable regulatory and scientific requirements.[25] A generic firm that files an ANDA including a paragraph III certification must, even after meeting pertinent regulatory and scientific requirements, wait for approval until the drug's listed patent expires.[26]

The filing of an ANDA application with a paragraph IV certification constitutes a "somewhat artificial" act of patent infringement under the Hatch-Waxman Act.[27] The statute requires the generic applicant to notify the proprietor of the patents that are the subject of a paragraph IV certification.[28] The patent owner may then commence patent infringement litigation against that applicant.

THE SAFE HARBOR PROVISION

The scope of 35 U.S.C. §271(e)(1) was recently the subject of judicial consideration. By its own terms, this statute does not restrict its infringement safe harbor to activities performed prior to the award of marketing approval by the FDA.[29] In the August 31, 2011, panel opinion in *Classen Immunotherapies LLC v. Biogen Idec*,[30] a three-judge panel of the Federal Circuit nonetheless concluded that this statute was "directed to premarketing approval of generic counterparts before patent expiration."[31] In view of this holding, activities not associated with the preparation of an NDA or ANDA are not shielded by the safe harbor, even though they lead to information that must be reported to the FDA.

The *Classen* litigation involved three patents directed towards methods of immunization. The accused infringement consisted in part of the defendants' participation in studies evaluating associations between childhood vaccinations and the risk of developing type 1 diabetes.[32] The accused infringers asserted that their participation in studies evaluating risks associated with different vaccination schedules was reasonably related to their regulatory obligation to review and report adverse events to the FDA.[33] The district court agreed with the defendants and held that they did not infringe due to the statutory safe harbor.

The Federal Circuit reversed this holding on appeal. The majority sided with the patent owner and rejected the contention of the accused infringers that they were protected by the 35 U.S.C. §271(e)(1) safe harbor. According to Judge Newman, in an opinion joined by Chief Judge Rader, the legislative history of the Hatch-Waxman Act indicated that Congress intended the safe harbor only to expedite FDA approval of generic drugs.[34] Further, every prior judicial analysis of the statute had addressed activities performed prior to the award of FDA marketing approval.[35] She therefore asserted that "statute does not apply to information that may be routinely reported to the FDA, long after marketing approval has been obtained."[36]

Judge Moore authored a dissenting opinion that would have applied 35 U.S.C. §271(e)(1) to the accused infringement. In her view, the statute included no language restricting its scope to pre-approval activity.[37] Further, in her opinion, the legislative history simply did not speak to whether the statute covered post-approval activity or not.[38] She also observed that the Supreme Court had consistently construed the safe harbor in an expansive manner.[39]

Approximately one year after the release of *Classen*, a different three-judge panel of the Federal Circuit issued the decision of *Momenta Pharmaceuticals, Inc. v. Amphastar Pharmaceuticals, Inc.*[40] The *Momenta* panel consisted of Chief Judge Rader, who was part of the majority in *Classen*; Judge Moore, who had dissented in that case; and a third jurist, Judge Dyk. The *Momenta* litigation involved a generic version of LOVENOX® (enoxaparin), a drug that prevents blood clots. Enoxaparin is an artificial version of the naturally occurring molecule heparin.

The Federal Circuit explained that unlike most drugs, heparin does not consist of a single defined molecule, but rather a heterogeneous mixture of molecules that differ in "the length of the polysaccharide chain" and the "component disaccharide units and the corresponding distribution of disaccharide unit sequences in the polysaccharide chains."[41] As a result, in order for a generic product to be considered equivalent to brand-name enoxaparin, the FDA required ANDA applicants to establish five "standards of identity," including equivalence in "disaccharide building blocks, fragment mapping, and sequence of oligosaccharide species."[42] After Amphastar received FDA approval to market generic enoxaparin, Momenta brought suit based upon its patented method of analyzing an enoxaparin sample for the presence or absence of a non-naturally occurring sugar. According to Momenta, Amphastar necessarily infringed its patent because the "FDA requires a generic manufacture[r] to include in its manufacturing process the analysis of each batch of its enoxaparin drug substance to confirm that ... [it] includes a 1,6- anhydro ring structure."[43]

This time writing for the majority, Judge Moore held that Amphastar's activities were shielded from liability for patent infringement by 35 U.S.C. §271(e)(1). She again observed that Supreme Court precedent took an expansive view of the Hatch-Waxman Act's safe harbor provision and that the statute included no language restricting its scope to pre-approval activity.[44]

She further distinguished the *Classen* case. According to Judge Moore, the information submitted by Amphastar was not "routinely reported to the FDA" as in *Classen.* Rather, the FDA required Amphastar to test each batch of generic enoxaparin before releasing it to the market.[45] In her view, post-approval activities that are "reasonably related to the development and submission of information under a Federal law which regulates the manufacture, use, or sale of drugs" fall within the scope of Hatch-Waxman safe harbor.[46]

Chief Judge Rader contributed a vigorous dissent. In his view, Congress intended 35 U.S.C. §271(e)(1) to permit only "a limited amount of pre-approval experiments to obtain FDA approval."[47] He believed that the holding in *Classen* was controlling and that the *Momenta* majority had strained to "come out the exact opposite way."[48] In his view, Amphastar's testing should not have been shielded by the statutory safe harbor.

The holdings in *Classen* and *Momenta* are arguably quite significant in terms of determining the impact of intellectual property law within the health sciences. The *Classen* majority expressed concerns about the potential breadth of the Hatch-Waxman Act's safe harbor provision. Via statute and regulation, the FDA receives a great deal of information from the pharmaceutical industry at all stages of the life cycles of particular products. If 35 U.S.C. §271(e)(1) were to apply to post-approval activities, then a potentially broad swath of activity could be conducted free of the patent system. The *Classen* majority appeared to doubt that Congress intended to limit the value of pharmaceutical patents to this extent.

On the other hand, the *Momenta* majority correctly observes that 35 U.S.C. §271(e)(1) is not restricted to pre-approval activities through its own wording. The extent to which jurists should employ legislative histories and their sense of congressional purposes when construing statutes has been the subject of a longstanding debate that exceeds the scope of this report.[49] In terms of public health policy, the dissenting view would potentially reduce patent barriers to compliance with FDA regulators. This result would arguably come at the expense of intellectual property rights and incentives to bring innovative drugs to market, however.

Were 35 U.S.C. §271(e)(1) to be confined to pre-approval activities, the statutory safe harbor would principally act to regulate the timing of patent litigation. The Hatch-Waxman Act exempts a generic firm from infringement suits as it prepares its ANDA. Once an ANDA is filed, however, 35 U.S.C. §271(e)(2) potentially allows a patent infringement lawsuit to commence. If there were no time limit placed upon resort to the safe harbor, no patent litigation would occur at all with respect to post-approval activities. This distinction possibly motivated the *Classen* majority ruling that limited 35 U.S.C. §271(e)(1) to pre-approval activities despite the statute's literal wording.

THE PATENT INFRINGEMENT PROVISION

Recent judicial developments have also impacted 35 U.S.C. §271(e)(2), the counterpart to the safe harbor provision. This provision has traditionally been understood to allow a patent infringement lawsuit once a generic firm files an ANDA with a paragraph IV certification. For example, the Supreme Court once described 35 U.S.C. §271(e)(2) as establishing "a highly artificial act of infringement that consists of submitting an ANDA ... containing the fourth type of certification that is in error as to whether commercial manufacture, use, or sale of the new drug (none of which, of course, has actually occurred) violates the relevant patent."[50]

The actual text of 35 U.S.C. §271(e)(2) does not seem to require the filing of a paragraph IV ANDA for a brand-name firm to bring a patent infringement lawsuit, however. That statute states in pertinent part:

> It shall be an act of infringement to submit ... an application ... for a drug ... if the purpose of such submission is to obtain approval under such Act to engage in the commercial manufacture, use, or sale of a drug or veterinary biological product claimed in a patent or the use of which is claimed in a patent before the expiration of such patent.

Whether a cause of action under 35 U.S.C. §271(e)(2) is predicated upon a paragraph IV certification or not holds notable consequences for the Hatch-Waxman system. If such a certification is not required, then the filing of an ANDA could lead to charges of infringement for patents that are not listed in the Orange Book. This state of affairs could potentially limit the ability of the Orange Book to identify patents that pertain to a particular pharmaceutical and also impact patent enforcement more generally—two factors that may possibly affect the availability of generic medications.

The litigation in *Abraxis Bioscience Inc. v. Navinta LLC51* recently highlighted this issue, although the court's disposition of the matter did not conclusively resolve the issue. Abraxis holds the NDA for Naropin® (ropivacaine), a drug used during surgical anesthesia and for acute pain management. Navinta subsequently filed an ANDA with the intention of producing a generic version of this medication. Abraxis had identified only a single patent for listing in the Orange Book, U.S. Patent No. 4,870,086. The '086 patent claims an isomer of ropivacaine hydrochloride monohydrate. Navinta's ANDA included a paragraph IV certification to the '086 patent.[52]

Upon receiving notice of Navinta's paragraph IV ANDA, Abraxis sued Navinta under 35 U.S.C. §271(e)(2). Abraxis brought suit under the '086 patent. But it also alleged infringement of two other patents: U.S. Patent Nos. 5,670,524 and 5,834,489. Each of these patents addresses methods of using ropivacaine for the treatment of pain. But neither was listed in the Orange Book at the time Navinta filed its ANDA.[53] Although Navinta argued that the two method patents should be removed from the litigation, the district court concluded that a lawsuit under 35 U.S.C. §271(e)(2) was appropriate even though neither one was identified in the Orange Book.[54]

Navinta appealed this and other rulings to the Federal Circuit. Navinta cited several cases from the Supreme Court and Federal Circuit that, in its view, held that 35 U.S.C. §271(e)(2) requires a paragraph IV certification on an Orange Book-listed patent. In response, Abraxis pointed to the text of 35 U.S.C. §271(e)(2), which does not state such a requirement. Abraxis also asserted that neither the Supreme Court nor the Federal Circuit has ever directly held that a paragraph IV certification is a prerequisite to suit under 35 U.S.C. §271(e)(2).

On appeal, the Federal Circuit acknowledged this issue but did not address it. The court of appeals instead resolved the dispute between Abraxis and Navinta on a different basis. Abraxis ultimately purchased all three asserted patents from several other firms through a complex series of transactions. However, at the time it filed suit against Navinta, Abraxis was not the actual owner of the patents due to a break in the chain of title. Because Abraxis therefore lacked standing to assert the patents on the date it filed suit, the Federal Circuit ruled that its complaint should be dismissed.[55]

This issue may yet be placed before the courts in the future. Because Abraxis currently owns all three asserted patents, it now possesses the ability to file an infringement suit against Navinta. Other firms may potentially assert patents that are not listed in the Orange Book under 35 U.S.C. §271(e)(2) as well.

The scope of 35 U.S.C. §271(e)(2) potentially holds important consequences for the Hatch-Waxman system. The Orange Book essentially serves as a patent clearinghouse that allows generic firms to identify the intellectual property rights that protect brand-name pharmaceuticals.

To assist in this role, the Hatch-Waxman Act requires NDA applicants to identify appropriate patents that the FDA subsequently places in the Orange Book.[56] Although the statute offers certain advantages to identifying relevant patents,[57] it establishes no fine or other penalty if a brand-name firm fails to do so. The ability of brand-name firms to assert unlisted patents under 35 U.S.C. §271(e)(2) may further decrease their incentives to comply with this statutory obligation.

On the other hand, 35 U.S.C. §271(e)(2) was designed to allow brand-name and generic firms to resolve their patent disputes in a prompt manner. Unlike most patent infringement lawsuits, which focus on a commercially available product, Hatch-Waxman litigation commences before the generic drug is publicly available and even before the FDA has approved the generic drug for marketing. This "head start" may allow the lawsuit to be resolved in a timelier manner. Under this system, litigation involving all pertinent patents—including ones not listed in the Orange Book— might best serve the goals of both the intellectual property and public health systems.

In this respect, it should be appreciated that the Hatch-Waxman Act states particular requirements for the sorts of patents that are appropriately listed in the Orange Book. The statute provides that an NDA applicant must identify to the FDA:

> any patent which claims the drug for which the applicant submitted the application or which claims a method of using such drug and with respect to which a claim of patent infringement could reasonably be asserted if a person not licensed by the owner engaged in the manufacture, use, or sale of the drug.[58]

Stated differently, the statute establishes two requirements for an Orange Book listing. First, the patent must claim a drug, or a method of using a drug, for which the applicant submitted the NDA. Second, the patent proprietor could reasonably assert a claim of infringement of that patent against a proposed generic version of the drug.[59]

Due to this two-part standard, merely because a patent cannot be listed in the Orange Book does not mean that the patent could not be successfully enforced against an unauthorized competitor. Patents claiming methods of manufacture, chemical intermediates, and product packaging are among those that may not be listed, even though they may possibly be infringed.[60] In such cases, exclusion from the Orange Book would not prevent the patent proprietor from bringing suit at such time the generic product was marketed.[61] Allowing litigation under 35 U.S.C. §271(e)(2) for unlisted patents would fulfill the policy goal of prompt resolution of pharmaceutical patent disputes—but also potentially place more intellectual property barriers to generic competition.

Congressional Issues and Options

Should Congress conclude that the current situation with respect to 35 U.S.C. §271(e) is satisfactory, no action need be taken. If Congress wishes to intervene, however, then some options present themselves. Congress could stipulate whether 35 U.S.C. §271(e)(1) applies to acts that occur following the award of FDA marketing approval or not. Congress could also explicitly state whether 35 U.S.C. §271(e)(2) establishes a cause of action for infringement of patents that have not been listed in the Orange Book and therefore were not the subject of a paragraph IV certification.

Recent interpretational disputes with respect to 35 U.S.C. §271(e) have drawn attention to potential distinctions between traditional Hatch-Waxman Act practice and the arguably broader wording of that statute. The courts commonly resolve these questions using traditional legal methods of statutory interpretation. But their rulings may significantly impact the two policy goals of the Hatch-Waxman Act: the preservation of incentives to develop innovative medications and the promotion of generic competition. Those who view the availability of new cures and the cost of health care as pressing issues of national importance would do well to track future judicial interpretation of these core Hatch-Waxman Act provisions.

End Notes

1 P.L. 84-417, 98 Stat. 1585 (1984).

2 See, e.g., Michael R. Herman, "The Stay Dilemma: Examining Brand and Generic Incentives for Delaying the Resolution of Pharmaceutical Patent Litigation," 111 Columbia Law Review (2011), 1788.

3 See Merck KGaA v. Integra Lifesciences I, Ltd., 545 U.S. 193, 202 (2005).

4 U.S. Department of Health and Human Services, Food and Drug Administration, Electronic Orange Book, Center for Drug Evaluation and Research, "Approved Drug Products with Therapeutic Evaluations" (available at http://www.accessdata.fda.gov/scripts/ cder/ob/ default.cfm).

5 21 U.S.C. §355(j)(5)(B)(iii).

6 Momenta Pharmaceuticals, Inc. v. Amphastar Pharmaceuticals, Inc., 686 F.3d 1348 (Fed. Cir. 2012); Classen Immunotherapies, Inc. v. Biogen Idec, 659 F.3d 1057 (Fed. Cir. 2011).

[7] 35 U.S.C. §271(e)(1) provides in pertinent part:

It shall not be an act of infringement to make, use, offer to sell, or sell within the United States ... a patented invention ... solely for uses reasonably related to the development and submission of information under a Federal law which regulates the manufacture, use, or sale of drugs or veterinary biological products.

[8] Eli Lilly v. Medtronic, 496 U.S. 661, 678 (1990) ("That is what is achieved by §271(e)(2)-the creation of a highly artificial act of infringement that consists of submitting an ANDA ... containing the fourth type of certification that is in error as to whether commercial manufacture, use, or sale of the new drug (none of which, of course, has actually occurred) violates the relevant patent.").

[9] 35 U.S.C. §271(e)(2) provides in pertinent part:

It shall be an act of infringement to submit ... an application ... for a drug ... if the purpose of such submission is to obtain approval under such Act to engage in the commercial manufacture, use, or sale of a drug or veterinary biological product claimed in a patent or the use of which is claimed in a patent before the expiration of such patent.

[10] 659 F.3d 1057 (Fed. Cir. 2011).

[11] 686 F.3d 1348 (Fed. Cir. 2012)

[12] See G. Lee Skillington & Eric M. Solovy, "The Protection of Test and Other Data Required by Article 39.3 of the TRIPS Agreement," 24 Northwestern Journal of International Law and Business (2003), 1.

[13] See Alfred B. Engelberg, "Special Patent Provisions for Pharmaceuticals: Have They Outlived Their Usefulness?," 39 IDEA: Journal of Law and Technology (1999), 389.

[14] See James J. Wheaton, "Generic Competition and Pharmaceutical Innovation: The Drug Price Competition and Patent Term Restoration Act of 1984," 34 Catholic University Law Review (1986), 433.

[15] See Kristin E. Behrendt, "The Hatch-Waxman Act: Balancing Competing Interest or Survival of the Fittest?," 57 Food & Drug Law Journal (2002), 247.

[16] Id.

[17] See, e.g., Justina A. Molzon, "The Generic Drug Approval Process," 5 Journal of Pharmacy & Law (1996), 275 ("The Act streamlined the approval process by eliminating the need for [generic drug] sponsors to repeat duplicative, unnecessary, expensive and ethically questionable clinical and animal research to demonstrate the safety and efficacy of the drug product.").

[18] See Jonathan M. Lave, "Responding to Patent Litigation Settlements: Does the FTC Have It Right Yet?," 64 University of Pittsburgh Law Review (2002), 201 ("Hatch-Waxman has also increased the generic drug share of prescription drug volume by almost 130% since its enactment in 1984. Indeed, nearly 100% of the top selling drugs with expired patents have generic versions available today versus only 35% in 1983.").

[19] Natalie M. Derzko, "A Local and Comparative Analysis of the Experimental Use Exception—Is Harmonization Appropriate?," 44 IDEA: Journal of Law and Technology (2003), 1.

[20] Merck KGaA v. Integra Lifesciences I, Ltd., 545 U.S. 193 (2005).

[21] 21 U.S.C. §355(b)(1).

[22] See, e.g., Jacob S. Wharton, "'Orange Book' Listing of Patents Under the Hatch-Waxman Act," 47 St. Louis University Law Journal (2003), 1027.

[23] 21 U.S.C. §355(j)(2)(A)(vii).

[24] See Douglas A. Robinson, "Recent Administrative Reforms of the Hatch-Waxman Act: Lower Prices Now In Exchange for Less Pharmaceutical Innovation Later?," 81 Washington University Law Quarterly (2003), 829.

[25] 21 U.S.C. §355(j)(5)(B)(i).
[26] 21 U.S.C. §355(j)(5)(B)(ii).
[27] Eli Lilly & Co. v. Medtronic, Inc., 496 U.S. 1047 (1990).
[28] 21 U.S.C. §355(j)(2)(B)(i).
[29] 35 U.S.C. §271(e)(1) provides in pertinent part:

It shall not be an act of infringement to make, use, offer to sell, or sell within the United States ... a patented invention ... solely for uses reasonably related to the development and submission of information under a Federal law which regulates the manufacture, use, or sale of drugs or veterinary biological products.

[30] 659 F.3d 1057 (Fed. Cir. 2011).
[31] Id. at 1071.
[32] Classen, 381 F.Supp.2d at 455.
[33] For example, 21 C.F.R. §600.80 requires "postmarketing reporting of adverse experiences" and 21 C.F.R. §601.70 requires "annual progress reports of postmarketing studies.
[34] 659 F.3d at 1071.
[35] Id.
[36] Id. at 1070.
[37] Id. at 1083.
[38] Id. at 1083-84.
[39] Id. at 1083.
[40] 686 F.3d 1348 (Fed. Cir. 2012).
[41] Id. at 1349.
[42] Id. at 1350.
[43] Id. at 1352.
[44] Id. at 1355.
[45] Id. at 1357-58.
[46] Id. at 1359.
[47] Id. at 1367.
[48] Id. at 1368.
[49] See, e.g., Antonin Scalia, A Matter of Interpretation: Federal Courts and the Law (Princeton University Press 1998).
[50] 496 U.S. 661, 678 (1990).
[51] 625 F.3d 1359 (Fed. Cir. 2010).
[52] 625 F.3d at 1360-61.
[53] Id. at 1361-62.
[54] Id. at 1362-63.
[55] Id. at 1365.
[56] 21 U.S.C. §355(b)(1).
[57] In particular, the FDA grant of marketing approval of a generic version of the patented drug may be delayed by 30 months. 21 U.S.C. §355(j)(5)(B)(iii).
[58] 21 U.S.C. §355(b)(1).
[59] John R. Thomas, Pharmaceutical Patent Law 404 (2d ed. Bureau of National Affairs 2010).
[60] See Department of Health and Human Services, Food and Drug Admin., Applications for FDA Approval to Market a New Drug: Patent Submission and Listing Requirements and Application of 30-Month Stays on Approval of Abbreviated New Drug Applications Certifying That a Patent Claiming a Drug Is Invalid or Will Not Be Infringed, 68 Fed. Reg. 36,676 (June 18, 2003).

[61] See aaiPharma, Inc. v. Thompson, 296 F.3d 227, 241 n.7, 63 USPQ2d 1670, 1679 n.7 (4th Cir. 2002) (noting that the owner of an unlisted patent "can still pursue patent infringement suits against generic manufacturers.").

In: Pharmaceutical Patents
Editor: Florian Aerts
ISBN: 978-1-62618-758-0

Chapter 4

THE HATCH-WAXMAN ACT: OVER A QUARTER CENTURY LATER*

Wendy H. Schacht and John R. Thomas

SUMMARY

Congressional interest in health-related issues has refocused attention on legislative efforts to provide both new as well as lower-cost pharmaceuticals for the marketplace. P.L. 98-417, the Drug Price Competition and Patent Term Restoration Act of 1984 (commonly known as the Hatch-Waxman Act), made significant changes to the patent laws as they apply to pharmaceutical products in an attempt to balance the need for innovative new drugs and the availability of less expensive generic products. The act created several practices intended to facilitate the marketing of generic drugs while permitting brand name companies to recover a portion of their intellectual property rights lost during the pharmaceutical approval process. Twenty-five years later, the impact of the act on the pharmaceutical industry may have implications for current congressional efforts to facilitate the development of new, inventive products while reducing costs to consumers.

Prior to the implementation of the Hatch-Waxman Act, 35% of top-selling drugs had generic competitors after patent expiration; now almost all do. The Generic Pharmaceutical Association points out that of 12,751

* This is an edited, reformatted and augmented version of a Congressional Research Service publication, CRS Report for Congress R41114, from www.crs.gov, prepared for Members and Committees of Congress, dated December 5, 2012.

drugs listed in the Orange Book, 10,072 have generic substitutes available to consumers. Concurrently, the time to market for these generic products has decreased substantially. According to the Congressional Budget Office, in 1984 the average time between the expiration of a patent on a brand name drug and the availability of a generic was three years. Today, upon FDA approval a generic may be introduced immediately after patents on the innovator drug expire as companies are permitted to undertake clinical testing during the time period associated patents are in force. In cases where the generic manufacturer is the patent holder, a substitute drug may be brought to market before the patent expires.

Industry support for pharmaceutical research and development has grown since the passage of the legislation although some recent figures indicate reduced R&D spending by several companies. In the absence of the research, development, and testing performed by the brand name pharmaceutical companies, generic drugs would not exist. The provisions of the Hatch-Waxman Act permit the generic industry to rely on information generated and financed by the brand name companies to obtain approval for their product by the FDA. However, the pharmaceutical industry today differs significantly from what it was in the early 1980s when the legislation was enacted. The cost of developing a drug has doubled, as has the number of clinical trials necessary to file a new drug application. The number of participants required for these trials has tripled. As the rate of return on investments in a new drug declined 12%, manufacturers often spend R&D dollars on developing improved versions of, or new delivery methods for an existing product.

Many experts agree that the Drug Price Competition and Patent Term Restoration Act has had a significant effect on the availability of generic substitutes for brand name drugs. Yet, congressional concerns remain whether or not the balance inherent in the act remains appropriate over 25 years later.

INTRODUCTION

Health-related issues before Congress have refocused attention on legislative efforts to provide both new as well as lower-cost pharmaceuticals for the marketplace. P.L. 98-417, the Drug Price Competition and Patent Term Restoration Act of 1984 (commonly known as the Hatch-Waxman Act),[1] made several significant changes to the patent laws as they apply to pharmaceutical products in an attempt to balance the need for innovative new drugs and the availability of less expensive generic products. Twenty-five years later, effects of the act on the pharmaceutical industry may have implications for current congressional efforts to facilitate the development of new, inventive products while reducing costs to consumers.

The Hatch-Waxman Act established several practices intended to facilitate the marketing of generic drugs while permitting brand name companies to recover a portion of their intellectual property rights lost during the pharmaceutical approval process. The legislative changes include methods for extending the term of a patent to reflect regulatory delays encountered in obtaining marketing consent from the FDA; a statutory exemption from patent infringement for activities associated with regulatory marketing approval for a generic version of a patented drug; establishment of mechanisms to challenge the validity of a pharmaceutical patent; and a reward for disputing the validity, enforceability, or infringement of a patented and approved drug. The act also affords the FDA certain authority to offer periods of data and marketing exclusivity for a pharmaceutical independent of the rights conferred by patents.

The provisions in the Hatch-Waxman Act differ from traditional infringement procedures associated with other patented products and processes. The company making a generic product is permitted to rely upon data paid for and compiled by the original manufacturer to establish the drug's safety and efficacy necessary to obtain FDA marketing approval. This expedited approval process may allow a bioequivalent drug to reach the market as soon as the patent on the original pharmaceutical expires. Nowhere else in U.S. patent law does such a robust "experimental use" exemption exist.

Overview of the Original Act

Accelerated Generic Drug Approval Process

Patents are issued by the United States Patent and Trademark Office (USPTO), generally for a term of 20 years from the date of filing. A patent grants its owner the right to exclude others from making, using, selling, offering to sell, or importing into the United States the patented invention. To be afforded patent rights, an invention must be judged to consist of patentable subject matter, possess utility, and be novel and nonobvious. The application must fully disclose and distinctly claim the invention for which protection is sought.

The grant of a patent does not provide the owner with an affirmative right to market the patented invention. Pharmaceutical products are also subject to marketing approval by the FDA. Federal laws typically require that pharmaceutical manufacturers show that their products are safe and effective in order to bring these drugs to the marketplace.[2] USPTO issuance of a patent and FDA marketing consent are distinct events that depend upon different criteria.

The Hatch-Waxman Act modified the 1952 Patent Act[3] by creating a statutory exemption from certain claims of patent infringement in the pharmaceutical sector. Generic manufacturers may commence work on a generic version of an approved brand name drug any time during the life of the patent, so long as that work furthers compliance with FDA regulations. Although the act provides a safe harbor from patent infringement, it also requires would-be manufacturers of generic drugs to engage in a specialized certification procedure. The core feature of this process is that a request for FDA marketing approval is treated as an "artificial" act of patent infringement. This action is intended to allow judicial resolution of the validity, enforceability, and infringement of patent rights afforded by the USPTO.

Under P.L. 98-417, each holder of an approved new drug application (NDA) is required to list patents it believes would be infringed if a generic drug were marketed before the expiration of these patents. The FDA maintains this list of patents in its publication, *Approved Drug Products with Therapeutic Equivalence Evaluations*, commonly known as the "Orange Book." The Orange Book provides generic pharmaceutical manufacturers with an accessible list of approved drugs that are potentially eligible for an "Abbreviated New Drug Application" (ANDA) or a "paper NDA" (a 505(b)(2) application). An ANDA or paper NDA permits the generic manufacturer to rely upon the safety and efficacy data of the original manufacturer when applying to the FDA for approval of a generic drug.

A generic firm must certify to the FDA its intentions with regard to each patent associated with the generic drug it seeks to market. Four possibilities exist under the 1984 Act: (1) that patent information on the drug has not been filed; (2) that the patent has already expired; (3) the date on which the patent will expire; or (4) that the patent is invalid or will not be infringed by the manufacture, use or sale of the drug for which the ANDA is submitted. These certifications are respectively termed paragraph I, II, III, and IV certifications. An ANDA certified under paragraphs I or II is approved immediately after meeting all applicable regulatory and scientific requirements. An ANDA certified under paragraph III must, even after meeting pertinent regulatory and scientific requirements, wait for approval until the drug's listed patent expires.

An ANDA applicant filing a paragraph IV certification must notify the proprietor of the patent. The patent holder may bring a patent infringement suit within 45 days of receiving such notification. If the patent owner timely brings a patent infringement charge against the ANDA applicant, then the FDA must suspend approval of the ANDA until (1) the date of the court's decision that the listed drug's patent is either invalid or not infringed; (2) the date the listed drug's patent expires, if the court finds the listed drug's patent infringed; or (3) subject to modification by the court, the date that is 30 months from the date the owner of the listed drug's patent received notice of the filing of a Paragraph IV certification.

Once the brand name company indicates an intent to bring a patent infringement suit against the generic company as a result of the paragraph IV filing, the FDA is prohibited from approving the drug in question for 30 months or until such time that the patent is found to be invalid or not infringed. If, prior to the expiration of 30 months, the court holds that the patent is invalid or would not be infringed, then the FDA will approve the ANDA when that decision occurs. Conversely, if the court holds the patent is not invalid and would be infringed by the product proposed in the ANDA prior to the expiration of 30 months, then the FDA will not approve the ANDA until the patent expires.

Under the original Hatch-Waxman Act, the first generic applicant to file a paragraph IV certification was awarded a 180-day market exclusivity period by the FDA as a reward for challenging the patent associated with an approved pharmaceutical. This provision was intended to encourage generic applicants to challenge a listed patent for an approved drug product. The 180-day market exclusivity period ordinarily began on the earliest of two dates: (1) the day the drug is first commercially marketed; or (2) the day a court decision holds that the patent which is the subject of the certification is invalid or not infringed. The interpretation of a "court decision" included the decision of a U.S. district court. A successful defense of a patent infringement suit was not necessary to obtain this exclusivity period.

Patent Term Restoration

The 1984 legislation also provides for the extension of patent term. Ordinarily, patent term is set to 20 years from the date the patent application is filed.[4] For pharmaceutical patents, the patent term may be extended for a portion of the time lost during clinical testing. More specifically, this term extension is equal to half of the time between the effective date of the investigational new drug application and the submission of the NDA, plus the entire time lost during FDA approval of the NDA.[5]

Certain caps on the length of the term restoration are established. The entire patent term restored may not exceed five years. Further, the remaining term of the restored patent following FDA approval of the NDA may not exceed 14 years.[6] The legislation also provides that the patentee must exercise due diligence to seek patent term restoration from the USPTO, or the period of lack of diligence will be offset from the augmented patent term.[7]

Patent term extension does not occur automatically. The patent owner or its agent must file an application with the USPTO requesting term extension within 60 days of obtaining FDA marketing approval. In addition, only one patent may be subject to term extension with respect to each FDA-approved product. In the event the NDA holder owns multiple patents that pertain to a particular approved drug, it must select one of them for term extension.

Data Exclusivity

Provisions that create data exclusivity for certain FDA-approved drugs are included in the legislation. The term "data exclusivity" refers to a period of time during which the FDA affords an approved drug protection from competing generic applications by limiting FDA's use of the innovator pharmaceutical's proprietary safety and efficacy information during the generic approval process for a specific period of time. A grant of data exclusivity does not depend on the existence of patent protection.

The length of data exclusivity is contingent on whether or not the drug is considered a new chemical entity (NCE). An NCE drug is defined as an approved drug which consists of active ingredients, including the ester or salt of an active ingredient, none of which has been approved in any other full NDA.[8]

If the approved drug is not an NCE, then the FDA may not approve an ANDA for a generic version of the approved drug until three years after the approval date of the pioneer NDA.[9]

In contrast, if the approved drug is an NCE, then a would-be generic manufacturer cannot submit an ANDA until five years after the date of the approval of the pioneer NDA.[10] The effect of this provision is to restrict a potential generic manufacturer from bringing a product to market for five years plus the length of the FDA review of the ANDA.

AMENDMENTS: THE MEDICARE PRESCRIPTION DRUG AND MODERNIZATION ACT OF 2003

Title XI of P.L. 108-173, the Medicare Prescription Drug and Modernization Act of 2003, as signed into law by the President on December 8, 2003, made several changes to the original Hatch-Waxman Act that were designed to decrease the time needed to bring generic pharmaceuticals to the marketplace. The new provisions were designed to "close some of the loopholes" critics argued that the brand name companies used to delay the introduction of generic products. The legislation permits only one automatic 30-month stay on FDA approval of drugs for which patents are listed in the Orange Book at the time of a paragraph IV ANDA or 505(b)(2) filing. The applicant may not amend the paragraph IV certification to include a drug different from that approved by the FDA, but may amend the application if seeking marketing consent for a different strength of the same drug. Modifications to the default 30-month stay are allowed based on district court judgments.

The applicant for an abbreviated new drug approval containing a paragraph IV certification must provide the brand name company and any patent owners with notice of such action within 20 days of filing with the FDA. Upon receipt of this notice, the brand name manufacturer has 45 days within which to file an infringement suit and thereby be eligible for the automatic 30-month stay.

In a situation where a patent holder does not file an infringement action within 45 days of notification of a paragraph IV ANDA, the ANDA applicant may request that a district court issue a declaratory judgment regarding the validity of the patent. In order to request a declaratory judgment, the generic manufacturer must have made available to the brand name company and the patent owners the confidential information contained in the ANDA application.

If sued, the generic firm may file a counter claim to require the patent holder make changes in the Orange Book listings. The generic firm may request that certain patents be delisted because they do not claim the drug to which they are attached. No monetary damages are to be awarded.

The Food and Drug Administration may approve the ANDA or 505(b)(2) filing containing a paragraph IV certification on the date of an appeals court decision, the date of a settlement order or consent decree, or when a district court decision is not appealed.

The 180-day market exclusivity is to begin with the first commercial marketing of the generic drug (rather than being triggered by a "court decision" as under the original legislation). This exclusivity can be forfeited in certain situations including failure to market under specific time constraints, withdrawal of the application, amendment of the certification, failure to obtain approval from the FDA, expiration of all patents, or the determination by the Federal Trade Commission or the Assistant Attorney General that an agreement between the brand name and generic firms violates antitrust laws. Subsequent applicants would not be permitted the 180-day exclusivity.

Multiple generic firms may qualify for the 180-day market exclusivity if several ANDA applicants file a substantially complete application on the same day.

Agreements tendered between brand name companies and generic firms concerning the production, sale, or marketing of a pharmaceutical or a 180-day market exclusivity must be filed with the Federal Trade Commission and the Department of Justice within 10 days of the agreement.

IMPLEMENTATION

Many experts agree that the Drug Price Competition and Patent Term Restoration Act has had a significant effect on the availability of generic substitutes for brand name drugs. Prior to the law, 35% of top-selling drugs had generic competitors after patent expiration; now almost all do.[11] The Generic Pharmaceutical Association (GPhA) points out that of 12,751 drugs listed in the Orange Book, 10,072 have generic substitutes available to consumers.[12] Concurrently, the time to market for these generic products has decreased substantially. According to the Congressional Budget Office (CBO), prior to passage of the act in 1984, the average time between the expiration of a brand name patent and the availability of a generic was three years. Today, upon FDA approval a generic may be introduced immediately after patents on the innovator drug expire, as companies are permitted to undertake clinical testing during the time period associated patents are in force. "By streamlining the approval process for a generic drug form, the Hatch-Waxman Act reduced the average delay between patent expiration and generic entry into the consumer market from *greater* than three *years* to *less* than three *months* for top-selling drugs."[13] In cases where the generic manufacturer is the patent holder, a substitute drug may be brought to market before the patent expires.

According to one analysis, 18.6% of U.S. prescriptions were written for generic products in 1984, the year the Hatch-Waxman Act was passed, while today they account for 63% of all U.S. prescriptions.[14] Similarly, CBO found that in 1980 13% of prescriptions for multi-source drugs were filled by generic prescriptions.[15] By 2009, GPhA maintains that 74.2% of prescriptions were filled by generics (65.6% by unbranded generics, 8.6% by generics produced or licensed by the brand name company).[16] The latest data from the IMS Institute for Healthcare Informatics demonstrate that in 2011, 80% of all retail prescriptions were filled by generics.[17]

While generics fill over two-thirds of written prescriptions, they represent a much smaller portion of the sales in the United States. According to GPhA, in 2009 unbranded generics generated 10.5% of U.S. pharmaceutical sales, branded generics generated 12.4% of sales, and brands generated 77.1% of total U.S. sales.[18] Later data from IMS Institute for Healthcare Informatics indicates that generics made up 27% of U.S. sales in 2011.[19] Projecting into the future, IMS argues that by 2016, 44% of 2011 spending on brand products in the U.S. market will shift to generic drugs.[20]

If generic versions of the brand pharmaceutical are easy to produce, multiple competitors often come to market at prices that are up to 80% below the innovator drug.[21] Studies have demonstrated that in the late 1980s a branded drug that went off patent would lose between 15% and 30% of sales volume within the first two years; in 2001 when Prozac faced generic competition, more than 70% of the market for the innovator pharmaceutical was lost within two months.[22] However, prices for generic drugs themselves tend to fall over time.[23] In addition, the market share of generic drugs is not just dependent on prices; other factors such as perception of quality, as well as first to market, may make a difference.[24]

Industry funding for pharmaceutical research and development has grown significantly since passage of the act in 1984. A Congressional Budget Office report notes that annual spending on R&D by drug companies has increased from approximately $8 billion in 1984 to $50 billion in 2008 (2008 constant dollars). In addition, the average increase in private sector R&D over the time period from 1980 to 2008 was almost 9% per year.[25]

However, other studies indicate that that R&D spending has recently declined. An analysis of the top 50 global pharmaceutical companies (as determined by their 2010 healthcare revenue) found that 18 of these firms, including AstraZeneca and GlaxoSmithKline, decreased their annual R&D spending from the previous year.[26] Similarly, research performed by CMR International noted that "R&D expenditure continued to drop in 2010 to an estimated three year low of $68 billion, which is in stark contrast to the growth rate leading up to 2008."[27] Research and development funding by members of the Pharmaceutical Research and Manufacturers Association (PhRMA) dropped an estimated 2.4% in 2011 from the record high spending the previous year.[28]

In the absence of the research, development, and testing performed by the brand name pharmaceutical companies, generic drugs would not exist. The provisions of the Hatch-Waxman Act permit the generic industry to rely on information generated and financed by the brand name companies to obtain approval for their product by the FDA. However, the pharmaceutical industry today differs from what it was in the early 1980s. The cost of developing a drug has doubled[29] to where it now takes over $1 billion to bring a new drug to market.[30] The cost of developing a generic is approximately $1 million to $2 million.[31] The number of clinical trials necessary to file a new drug application has doubled since 1980 and the number of participants in these trials has tripled.[32] Thus, the rate of return from investment in a new drug has dropped by 12% over this time period.[33]

Concurrently, companies appear to be moving away from the development of drugs that address large patient populations, but for which they cannot charge high prices, toward more specialized medicines, primarily biologics, that may be used by fewer patients, but for which high prices can be secured. In 2007, 55 blockbuster drugs were considered specialized products, up from 12 in 2001.[34] In 2011, 25% of total U.S. spending for traditional medicines was for specialty products.[35]

> "Thus, the specialty category continues to be a major focus of new drug development and comprises a significant percentage of new approvals."[36]

Since passage of the Hatch-Waxman Act, the number of patents on each marketed pharmaceutical has increased such that "to shield themselves against competition, manufacturers now carry an average of 10 patents for each drug—as compared with an average of 2 a decade ago."[37] Similarly, manufacturers are spending R&D dollars to develop new and improved forms of the original drug or new delivery methods (for example extended release tablets, liquid formulations) as related patents expire. The new version of the drug can be patented and users encouraged to switch to the new product.[38] According to PriceWaterhouseCoopers, "In 2007, only eight of the 27 new therapies launched worldwide were the first of their kind.... More than half were 'me-too' treatments with at least three predecessors."[39] Another study found that

> in 2004, more than 20% of the money 10 of the [world's] largest pharmaceutical companies invested in R&D went to line extensions and other work, as distinct from new development projects. In smaller companies, the percentage was over 40%.[40]

Between 1988 and 2006, over 500 pharmaceuticals received patent term extensions.[41] In 2006, 26 of the 40 top selling drugs in the United States had patent terms restored. During the patent restoration period, about 20% of gross revenues may be generated.[42] With the extension provided by the Hatch-Waxman Act, total time on the market prior to generic competition has been estimated at 11.5 years for drugs with annual sales of more than $100 million.[43] Additional research indicates

> (a) that newly approved NCEs have come on to the market with about eight to ten years of effective patent life or market exclusivity, and (b) that since 1997 the average exclusivity periods for newly approved NCEs have declined.[44]

Despite the extension of patent protection afforded by the legislation, many drugs will soon lose patent protection.[45] PriceWaterhouseCoopers notes that in 2006, 90% of revenues generated by the large pharmaceutical companies came from drugs that were on the market for more than five years and were therefore rapidly moving toward generic competition.[46] The estimates on the amount of sales lost by brand name companies when a drug loses patent protection vary. PriceWaterhouseCoopers argues that "the leading pharmaceutical companies will lose between 14% and 41% of their existing revenues as a result of patent expiries [sic],"[47] which exposes "an estimated $157 billion worth of sales (measured in 2005 dollars) to generic competition."[48] EvaluatePharma puts the amount of U.S. sales affected by patent expirations between 2011 and 2016 at $133 billion; 2012 is expected to be the most severe with $33.2 billion in sales affected.[49] The results of subsequent generic entry can be dramatic:

> As more [generic] competitors enter the field, prices drop even further. For example, almost as soon as GlaxoSmithKline's popular cardiovascular drug Coreg ($1.7 billion in US sales for the 12 months

trailing June 2007, according to IMS Health, Inc.) lost patent protection in September 2007, more than a dozen generic competitors entered the market, causing prices to fall immediately and dramatically. Within a month, generics accounted for 85% of the Coreg market, with prices substantially lower than those of the branded product prior to its patent expiration.[50]

While there are various compilations of drugs that are expected to go off patent, it is apparent that many innovator pharmaceuticals will be affected. Lipitor, the world's best-selling drug, lost patent protection at the close of 2011. Among the 2011 top selling drugs in the U.S. market that went off patent in 2012 are Plavix ($5.7 billion), Singulair ($4.4 billion), Seroquel ($3.8 billion), Actos ($2.8 billion), Lexapro ($2.7 billion), and Diovan/Diovan HCT ($1.7 billion and $1.5 billion respectively).[51] Other drugs that are expected to lose patent protection in the near future include Cymbalta (2011 U.S. sales of $3.4 billion), Nexium (2011 U.S. sales of $5.5 billion), Celebrex ($1.6 billion), Nasonex ($1.1 billion), Abilify ($4.8 billion), Enbrel (2011 U.S. sales of $1.3 billion), Crestor ($3.9 billion) and Humira ($1.3 billion).[52]

The loss of patent protection on these drugs is occurring at a time when some experts claim that innovation and productivity has stalled in the pharmaceutical industry. According to Jean-Pierre Garnier, chief executive officer of GlaxoSmithKline, the value of "Big Pharma" is diminishing because of declining R&D productivity.[53] The pharmaceutical industry is particularly research intensive. In 2011, total worldwide spending on R&D was estimated at $135 billion, with 18.8% of sales reinvested in R&D according to EvaluatePharma.[54] Members of PhRMA invested 21.1% of domestic sales in domestic R&D during 2011.[55] The Congressional Budget Office reports that "pharmaceutical firms invest as much as five times more in research and development, relative to their sales, than the average U.S. manufacturing firm."[56] However, while pharmaceutical R&D expenditures have increased substantially over the past 15 years, drug approvals have remained relatively flat.[57] Research by Standard & Poors found that there is

> a relative dearth of innovative new products launched in recent years relative to funds invested in R&D. According to the Pharmaceutical Research and Manufacturers Association ... US drug industry R&D spending expanded 30% from 2004 through 2008. Yet, the number of FDA-approved new molecular entities (NMEs) and novel biologics declined to 24 from 36 over the same period. This attrition occurred

> despite important advances in R&D technology platforms, such as rational drug design and genomics, that occurred earlier in the decade.[58]

In addition to a decline in the number of new drug approvals, there is concern in the healthcare community that the number of products in the pipeline are insufficient to make up for losses to generics after patent expiration. According to one analysis, only 4 of the 10 major pharmaceutical companies have drugs in clinical trials that are "sufficiently valuable to offset these losses."[59] The scarcity of new products in clinical trials may be a result of a situation that

> as more targets are discovered, the body of knowledge required to understand them, let alone use them for new therapies, increases dramatically, which delays the time when new or better therapies become available. In short, there can be sharply diminishing returns in drug R&D.[60]

Other experts maintain that counting NMEs is not an accurate measure of productivity. It is argued that the number of NME approvals has remained stable over the long term despite year to year changes. While R&D investments have increased, between 25% and 30% of R&D spending is directed at finding new indications for existing products. Thus, basing an assessment of decreased productivity on the number of new NMEs may not be accurate since a significant portion of the R&D spending has led to increased use of already approved drugs.[61]

An additional explanation for the slowdown in new drug approvals may be that the "easy" drugs have been developed. The targets of new pharmaceuticals are more complex and chronic diseases that require more complicated clinical trials.[62] The time frame between research and the introduction of a product in the marketplace tends to be particularly long in the pharmaceutical arena. Experts maintain that it generally takes 12 to 15 years to bring a new drug from discovery to market.[63] The basic research leading to discovery may even begin many years prior to discovery. Therefore, it is argued, any productivity gap is short-term as new drugs move toward approval.[64] According to Boston University's Iain Cockburn,

> These concerns about productivity are almost surely overblown: if past experience is any guide, the recent surge in R&D spending should generate a commensurate increase in new drug approvals of the next three

to ten [years].... Today's new drugs are the result of R&D expenditures stretching back decades into the past, and undertaken by many different institutions.[65]

SELECTED ISSUES

The implementation of the provisions of the Hatch-Waxman Act has raised several issues that have become the focus of congressional discussion. Among these concerns are an increase in the introduction of "authorized generics" marketed by brand name companies in response to the loss of revenue that accompanies the introduction of a generic product. Additionally, patent-related litigation has been replaced in certain situations by settlements between brand name and generic firms that include payments to the generic company in exchange for an agreement not to market the product. Concurrently, Congress is considering legislation to extend the act's accelerated marketing approach to biologic drugs. These issues are discussed briefly below; a detailed analysis of each can be found in the referenced CRS reports.

Authorized Generics[66]

An "authorized generic" is a pharmaceutical that is marketed by or on behalf of a brand name drug company, but is sold under a generic name.[67] Authorized generics are thus similar to "private label" products, which are manufactured by one firm but sold under the brand of another. Either the innovator drug company can authorize another firm to make a generic version of their product or the company can manufacture its own generic. The arrangement to offer an authorized generic is often made at the point where patent protection is soon to be lost. The authorized version may be brought to the market prior to or on the same day as a generic drug approved by the FDA and manufactured by a company that has won a paragraph IV challenge. Such arrangements allow the innovator firm to recover some of the sales income on a drug that will become widely available in generic form. According to GPhA, in 2007, 9.3% of prescriptions filled by generic drugs were filled by branded generics, which accounted for 10.3% of generic sales.[68]

There are potential benefits and costs to the consumer of these actions. On the one hand, authorized generics may dissuade other firms from filing paragraph IV challenges to brand name patents if the often significant financial investments can not be recouped through the 180-day market exclusivity period. Thus, potentially invalid patents may delay the introduction of a generic version of certain pharmaceuticals. Conversely, even brand name authorized generics are less expensive than the innovator drug and often can be made available prior to patent expiration. In addition, through the introduction of an authorized generic, two lower cost products can be made available to the consumer. While research shows these actions may adversely affect the generic company, the brand name firm and the public benefit.[69]

Authorized generics practice has proven controversial due to the Hatch-Waxman Act's architecture and incentive structures. Some commentators have voiced concerns that the introduction of authorized generics, particularly during the 180-day market exclusivity granted to the independent generic firm that brought a paragraph IV challenge, thwarts the policy goal of encouraging the introduction of generic pharmaceuticals.[70] In particular, critics argue that the use of authorized generics may discourage firms from filing paragraph IV patent challenges if their litigation expenses cannot be recouped through the 180-day market exclusivity period.[71] As antitrust attorney David A. Balto explains:

> The bounty from challenging a patent is very important. Pharmaceutical patent litigation is a multimillion-dollar proposition. But for the potential reward of six-month exclusivity that represents the vast majority of potential profits from generic entry, many firms might forgo challenging patents.[72]

For example, the FDA ruled that the generic manufacturer Apotex was entitled to 180-day exclusivity for its version of the anti-depressant drug Paxil® in 2003. The brand name drug company, GlaxoSmithKline, introduced an authorized generic version of Paxil®. Although Apotex anticipated sales of up to $575 million during the 180-day generic exclusivity period, its sales were reported to be between $150 million and $200 million.[73] In a 2004 filing with the FDA, attorneys for Apotex asserted "that the authorized generic crippled Apotex's 180-day exclusivity—it reduced Apotex's entitlement to about two-thirds—to the tune of approximately $400 million."[74]

In addition, brand name firms commonly introduce authorized generics on the eve of generic competition. Without an independent generic patent challenger in the first instance, brand name firms may themselves make diminished, or delayed, use of the authorized generic strategy. As a result, the pro-competitive benefits of authorized generics may be postponed, or not realized at all, should independent generic rivals become less willing to challenge patents held by brand name firms.[75]

On the other hand, authorized generics potentially offer several benefits both to drug companies and to consumers. Authorized generics are commonly less expensive than the brand name drug. The introduction of an authorized generic therefore allows a lower-cost product to be made available to the consumer.[76] As the FDA opined in a statement issued in July 2004:

> Marketing of authorized generics increases competition, promoting lower prices for pharmaceuticals, particularly during the 180-day exclusivity period in which the prices for generic drugs are often substantially higher than after other generic products are able to enter the market.[77]

In addition, once a generic version of a drug becomes available following patent expiration, brand name firms may lose considerable market share. Indeed, many health management organizations and insurance companies reportedly promote the use of generic substitutes for brand-name medications once they become available.[78] Absent participation in the generic market, brand name firms may not be able to take advantage of investments they previously made with respect to their manufacturing facilities. Authorized generics therefore allow brand name firms to continue to employ their manufacturing facilities at or near peak capacity even following patent expiration.[79]

Authorized generics may also support the research and development efforts of brand name firms by providing them with additional revenue. Authorized generics may supply the brand name firm with an additional income source, such as a royalty on sales made by its generic subsidiary or contracting partner.[80] These funds, or some portion of them, can potentially be employed in support of pharmaceutical innovation.

Authorized generics may also facilitate settlement of patent infringement suits between brand name and independent generic firms. A judicial holding of patent invalidity may have a severe impact upon a brand name firm in terms of its lost revenue. Many observers also believe that patent litigation is an uncertain venture.[81] By settling patent litigation, and allowing an ANDA applicant to produce an authorized generic, brand name firms may potentially better manage risk.

Such a technique provides a more stable revenue stream, both in support of the brand name firm's research and development activities and for its investors. The generic company making an authorized generic can also benefit by not having to expend funds on litigation with an uncertain outcome or pursue an ANDA at the FDA, while expanding its product line, acquiring manufacturing experience, and gaining the first-mover advantage in the generic market.[82]

The use of authorized generics as a litigation settlement mechanism also impacts consumers, but in a manner that is both less certain and likely varies on a case-by-case basis. On one hand, particular settlement agreements may provide for the sale of authorized generics years before the disputed patent is set to expire. As a result, consumers may gain early access to a lower-cost alternative to the brand name drug. On the other hand, had the generic firm refused to settle and ultimately prevailed in the litigation, then the market would have been open to full competition even earlier. The impact upon competition of a litigation settlement likely depends upon a number of complex factors, including the strength of the patent, the number of potential generic competitors, and the precise terms of the litigation settlement agreement.

Patent Settlements[83]

Brand name and generic firms engaged in litigation within the Hatch-Waxman statutory framework have sometimes concluded their litigation through settlement, rather than await a formal decision from a court. A few of these settlements have called for the brand name company to pay the generic firm in exchange for the generic firm's agreement not to market the patented pharmaceutical. These arrangements have been termed "reverse payment" agreements because they are contrary to the usual situation in patent infringement settlements, where the plaintiff-patentee receives money from the accused patent infringer.[84]

"Reverse payment" settlements potentially had significant market consequences prior to the enactment of P.L. 108-173. Under the old law, such an arrangement could sometimes prevent all other generic firms from entering the market. The reason is that the first generic challenger was entitled to a 180-day exclusivity against other generic firms that could not be revoked or forfeited. If the first generic challenger chose not to market at all, then no generic versions of a drug could be approved by the FDA until such time as the patent expired.[85]

Amendments to the original Hatch-Waxman Act contained in P.L. 108-173 include two provisions that make "reverse payment" arrangement less likely to occur in the future. First, settlement agreements between brand name and generic firms must, in many cases, be filed with the Federal Trade Commission and the Department of Justice. This provision allows the FTC and DOJ to review the settlements for anticompetitive effects. Second, P.L. 108-173 establishes various events that cause the first generic challenger to forfeit its 180-day exclusivity. Other generic firms will therefore be less easily shut out of the market in the future in the event that the first generic challenger opts not to market a particular drug.

Notably, certain "reverse payment" settlements reached under the old law have been subject to scrutiny under the antitrust laws. Enacted with the goal of preserving a competitive, open market, the antitrust laws make illegal a variety of practices that restrain trade and reduce consumer choices. Both the FTC and private plaintiffs have succeeded in persuading the federal courts that particular "reverse payment" settlements constitute antitrust violations. Different federal courts have reached conflicting rulings, however, on whether "reverse payment" settlements should automatically be considered to violate the antitrust laws,[86] or whether they should be subjected to a detailed, case-by-case review to determine whether the settlement was sufficiently anti-competitive to constitute an antitrust violation.[87] These rulings may have considerable impact upon the extent to which the antitrust laws will be used to monitor past conduct by different actors within the pharmaceutical industry. The U.S. Supreme Court may choose to resolve these conflicting views by issuing a ruling that would be binding upon the lower courts.[88]

Follow-On Biologics[89]

The accelerated market approval process for chemical, small molecule pharmaceuticals created by the Hatch-Waxman Act does not apply to biologic drugs.[90] Today, 20% of the drugs on the market are biologics[91] and many more new biologics reportedly are in the pipeline and/or in the approval process.[92] Projections are that by 2010, 50% of approved pharmaceuticals will be the result of biotechnology.[93] This sector is highly innovative, invests extensively in research and development, and is instrumental in providing products that contribute to the health and wellbeing of the nation. Observers agree that the biologics market is rapidly expanding by any number of measures, including the quantity of approved products, the size of the market, and the importance of these drugs to the health of U.S. citizens.

Awareness of the increasing importance of biopharmaceuticals has been accompanied by an appreciation that patents covering many of these products will soon expire. Estimates vary on the number of biologics that will lose patent protection in the next several years and the amount of sales these products represent. One study notes that "between 2009 and 2019, 21 blockbuster biopharmaceuticals with a total market value of over 50 billion $US will lose patent protection."[94] Analysis by FierceBiotech estimates that biologics worth $25 billion in sales will lose patent protection by 2016.[95] A report by PriceWaterhouseCoopers notes that between 2002 and 2013, the expiration of patents on blockbuster biopharmaceutical products will lead to an average loss of $16.4 billion in sales.[96]

While in the traditional pharmaceutical market, generic versions commonly become available to consumers as patents on brand name drugs expire due to the provisions of the Hatch-Waxman Act, Congress was concerned that loss of patent protection for biologics would not be accompanied by the introduction of competing, lower-cost products.[97] Biologics differ significantly from traditional pharmaceuticals in their complexity and method of manufacture. Typical pharmaceutical products consist of small molecules, on the order of dozens of atoms, that may be readily characterized and reproduced through well-understood chemical processes. In contrast, biologics are often made up of millions of atoms, feature a more complex structure than traditional pharmaceuticals, and are manufactured from living cells through biological processes.[98] As a result, the technical challenges that a competitor faces in developing a product that may be viewed as equivalent to a particular brand-name biologic product may be considerable, and in some cases perhaps even insurmountable.[99] For this reason, many experts do not describe competing biologic products as "generics," as is the case for a small-molecule pharmaceuticals; the terms "follow-on biologic" or "biosimilar" are commonly used instead.[100]

Some commentators asserted that these technical challenges also meant that the expedited approval pathways available under the Hatch-Waxman Act did not comfortably apply to biologics, most of which are approved under provisions of the Public Health Services Act (PHS Act). Because the complexity of biologics is an order of magnitude greater than that associated with pharmaceuticals, they say, an expedited marketing approval protocol would not ensure patient safety to the degree possible with respect to traditional drugs.[101] Other experts observed that different kinds of biologics vary considerably in their size and structure, and that existing Hatch-Waxman mechanisms provided appropriate regulatory oversight for less complex biologics and therefore should be extended to those biologics approved under the PHS Act. These observers further argued that as scientific knowledge progresses, understanding of biologics will increase, thereby allowing expanded use of then existing procedures.[102]

The 111th Congress turned to these concerns when it enacted the Biologics Price Competition and Innovation Act (BPCIA) of 2009, incorporated into Title VII of the Patient Protection and Affordable Care Act.[103] BPCIA established a licensure pathway for competing versions of previously marketed biologics. In particular, the legislation established a regulatory regime for two sorts of follow-on biologics, termed "biosimilar" and "interchangeable" biologics. The Food and Drug Administration (FDA) was afforded a prominent role in determining the particular standards for biosimilarity and interchangeability for individual products.

In addition, the legislation created FDA-administered periods of data protection and marketing exclusivity for certain brand-name drugs and follow-on products. Brand-name biologic products receive 4 years of marketing exclusivity and 12 years of data protection. The BPCIA also provides for a term of marketing exclusivity for the applicant that is the first to establish that its product is interchangeable with the brand-name product. Finally, the BPCIA created a patent dispute resolution procedure for use by brand-name and follow-on biologic manufacturers.

CONCLUSION

The Hatch-Waxman Act has been instrumental in providing patients with lower-cost generic copies of brand name drugs often the day that patents expire on the original product. At the same time, investment in pharmaceutical research and development has increased in real terms at an average of almost 9% a year. While the original legislation was amended in 2003 to address what were perceived as loopholes in the process, concerns still remain whether or not the balance achieved by the act remains appropriate over 25 years later. However, congressional legislation extending a similar accelerated marketing approach to biologic drugs may be indicative of a belief in the overall success of the Hatch-Waxman Act.

End Notes

[1] 21 U.S.C. §355 and following.
[2] 21 U.S.C. §355(b).
[3] P.L. 82-593; 35 U.S.C. §1 and following.
[4] 35 U.S.C. §156. Prior to United States adherence to the World Trade Organization, patents were granted a term of 17 years from the date of issuance. On June 8, 1995, the effective patent term was changed to 20 years measured from the date the patent application was filed. Patents in existence as of June 8, 1995, or patents that issued from applications pending at the USPTO as of the date, have a term equal to the greater of 17 years from issuance or 20 years from grant.
[5] 35 U.S.C. §156.
[6] 35 U.S.C. §156(c).
[7] 35 U.S.C. §156(d)(2)(B).
[8] 21 U.S.C. §355(j)(4)(D)(i).
[9] 21 U.S.C. §355(j)(4)(D)(iii).
[10] 21 U.S.C. §355(j)(D)(ii).
[11] Michael A. O'Shea and Christopher M. Mikson, "The Hatch-Waxman Act: Still Critical, Still in Flux," The National Law Journal, January 23, 2006.
[12] Generic Pharmaceutical Association, Facts at a Glance, available at http://www.gphaonline.org/about-gpha/aboutgenerics/facts.
[13] David A. Holdford and Bryan A. Liang, The Growing Influence of Generic Drugs: What it Means to Pharmacists and Physicians, Power-Pak C.E., December 2006, available at http://www.centad.org/seminar/4.%20Generics/ GrowingInfluencePowewrPak2006.pdf.
[14] Richard G. Frank, "The Ongoing Regulation of Generic Drugs," The New England Journal of Medicine, November 15, 2007, 1993.
[15] Congressional Budget Office, How Increased Competition from Generic Drugs Has Affected Prices and Returns in the Pharmaceutical Industry, (Washington, DC, July 1998), available at http://www.cbo.gov.
[16] Generic Pharmaceutical Association, Generics, A Steady Course in a Sea of Change, 2010, 17, available at http://www.gphaonline.org/sites/default/files/ Annual%20Report%202010. pdf.
[17] IMS Institute for Healthcare Informatics, The Use of Medicines in the United States: Review of 2011, April 2012, 26, available at http://www.theimsinstitute.org.
[18] Ibid.
[19] The Use of Medicines in the United States: Review of 2011, 26.
[20] IMS Institute for Healthcare Informatics, The Global Use of Medicines: Outlook Through 2016, July 2012, 24, available at http://www.theimsinstitute.com.
[21] Herman Saftlas, "Industry Surveys, Healthcare: Pharmaceuticals," Standard & Poor's, June 4, 2009, 29, available at http://www.standardandpoors.com.
[22] Richard G. Frank, "Regulation of Generic Drugs," The New England Journal of Medicine, August 30, 2007, 842.
[23] Henry G. Grabowski and John M. Vernon, "Brand Loyalty, Entry, and Price Competition in Pharmaceuticals After the 1984 Act," Journal of Law and Economics, October 1992, 347.
[24] Ibid.
[25] Congressional Budget Office, "Pharmaceutical R&D and the Evolving Market for Prescription Drugs," Economic and Budget Issue Brief, October 26, 2009, 3.

[26] Top 50 Pharmaceutical Companies and Their Pipelines 2011, PharmaLive.com Special Report, September 2011, 1 and 4, available at http://www.pharmalive.com/special_reports/sample.cfm?reportID=359.

[27] CMR International, "2011 Pharmaceutical R&D Factbook," as noted in Drug Dropout in Clinical Trials is at Unsustainable Levels, According to Thomson Reuters, CMR International, June 27, 2011 Press Release, available at http://thomsonreuters.com/content/press_room/science/R+D-CMR-factbook-2011.

[28] PhRMA, Pharmaceutical Industry 2012 Profile, inside front cover, available at http://www.phrma.org/sites/default/ files/159/phrma_industry_profile.pdf.

[29] The Hatch-Waxman Act: Still Critical, Still in Flux.

[30] Christopher Paul Adams and Van Vu Brantner, "Spending on New Drug Development," Health Economics, (published online 26 Feb.2009) Epub ahead of print.

[31] Henry Grabowski, "Patents, Innovation and Access to New Pharmaceuticals," Journal of International Economic Law, 2002, 852, available at http://jiel.oxfordjournals.org/cgi/reprint/5/4/849, and Henry Grabowski, "Patents and New Product Development in the Pharmaceutical and Biotechnology Industries," in Science and Cents: Exploring the Economics of Biotechnology, Proceedings of a 2002 Conference sponsored by the Federal Reserve Bank of Dallas, 90, available at http://www.dallasfed.org/research/pubs/science/grabowski.pdf

[32] Gregory J. Glover, "The Influence of Market Exclusivity on Drug Availability and Medical Innovations," The AAPS Journal, August 3, 2007, E313.

[33] The Hatch-Waxman Act: Still Critical, Still in Flux.

[34] PriceWaterhouseCoopers, Pharma 2020: Marketing the Future, February 2009, 13, available at http://www.pwc.com/pharma.

[35] IMS Institute for Healthcare Informatics, The Use of Medicines in the United States: Review of 2011, April 2012, 27, available at http://www.theimsinstitute.org.

[36] Medco, 2011 Drug Trend Report, 42, available at http://www.drugtrendreport.com/2011-report.

[37] The Ongoing Regulation of Generic Drugs, 1994.

[38] Ibid.

[39] Pharma 2020: Marketing the Future, 11.

[40] PriceWaterhouseCoopers, Pharma 2020: The Vision, June 2007, 8, available at http://www.pwc.com/pharma.

[41] Charles Clift, "The value of patent term extensions to the pharmaceutical industry in the USA," Journal of Generic Medicines, April 2008, 201.

[42] Ibid, 207-208.

[43] Pharmaceutical Research and Manufactures Association, Key Industry Facts About PhRMA, available at http://www.phrma.org/key_industry_facts_about_phrma.

[44] James W. Hughes, Michael J. Moore, and Edward A. Snyder, "Napsterizing" Pharmaceuticals: Access, Innovation, and Consumer Welfare, National Bureau of Economic Research, October 2002, 7, available at http://www.nber.org/ papers/w9229.

[45] For additional discussion see CRS Report R42399, Drug Patent Expirations: Potential Effects on Pharmaceutical Innovation, by Wendy H. Schacht.

[46] Pharma 2020: The Vision, 6.

[47] Ibid., 9.

[48] Ibid., 6.

[49] EvaluatePharma, Patent Storm Gathering Strength, January 28, 2011, available at http://www.evaluatepharma.com/ Universal/View.aspx?type=Story&id=235841&isEPVantage=yes.

[50] Industry Surveys, Healthcare: Pharmaceuticals, 29.

[51] Data derived from Express Scripts/Medco, Estimated Dates of Possible First time Generic/Rx-to-OTC Market Entry, June 2012, available at https://host1.medcohealth.com/art/ corporate/ anticipatedfirsttime_generics.pdf; Express Scripts/Medco, First-time Approved Generics: 2012*, August 13, 2012, available at https://host1.medcohealth.com/art/ corporate/ firsttime_generics.pdf; and Food and Drug Administration, Original Abbreviated New Drug Application (ANDA) Approvals, available at http://www.fda.gov.

[52] Estimated Dates of Possible First time Generic/Rx-to-OTC Market Entry, June 2012.

[53] Jean-Pierre Garnier, "Rebuilding the R&D Engine in Big Pharma," Harvard Business Review, May 1, 2008, 70.

[54] EvaluatePharma, World Preview 2018, Embracing the Patent Cliff, June 2012, 15, available at https://www.evaluatepharma.com/secure/FileResourceDownload.aspx?id=98a75eab-95f6-41d8-903f-4732848fdf78.

[55] Pharmaceutical Industry 2012 Profile, inside front cover.

[56] Congressional Budget Office, Research and Development in the Pharmaceutical Industry, October 2006, 9.

[57] Ernst & Young, Beyond Borders, Global Biotechnology Reports 2008, 18, available at http://www.ey.com/ beyondborders.

[58] Industry Surveys, Healthcare: Pharmaceuticals, 16.

[59] PriceWaterhouseCoopers, Pharma 2020: Virtual R&D, June 2008, 2, available at http://www.pwc.com.

[60] Fabio Pammolli and Massimo Riccaboni, "Market Structure and Drug Innovation," Health Affairs, January/February 2004, 49.

[61] William S. Comanor, "The Economics of Research and Development in the Pharmaceutical Industry, " in Frank A. Sloan and Chee-Ruey Hsieh, eds, Pharmaceutical Innovation, (Cambridge University Press, 2007), 66-67.

[62] Beyond Borders, Global Biotechnology Report 2008, 18.

[63] John A. Vernon, Testimony at Hearings on Prescription Drug Price Inflation: Are Prices Rising Too Fast?, House Committee on Energy and Commerce, December 8, 2009, 4 and Congressional Budget Office, "Pharmaceutical R&D and the Evolving Market for Prescription Drugs," Economic and Budget Issue Brief, October 26, 2009, 4.

[64] Boston Consulting Group, Rising to the Productivity Challenge, A Strategic Framework for Biopharma, July 2004, 4, available at http://www.bcg.com/documents/file14392.pdf.

[65] Iain Cockburn, Blurred Boundaries: Tensions Between Open Scientific Resources and Commercial Exploitation of Knowledge in Biomedical Research, April 30, 2005, 2, available at http://people.bu.edu/cockburn/cockburn-blurredboundaries.pdf.

[66] For a detailed discussion see CRS Report RL33605, Authorized Generic Pharmaceuticals: Effects on Innovation, by John R. Thomas.

[67] Leila Abboud, "'Authorized Generics' Duel Grows," Wall Street Journal, March 25, 2004 and Leila Abboud, "Drug Makers Use New Tactic to Ding Generic-Drug Firms," Wall Street Journal January 27, 2004.

[68] Generic Pharmaceutical Association Annual Report, 24.

[69] Morton I. Kamien and Israel Zang, "Virtual Patent Extension by Cannibalization," Southern Economic Journal, July 1999.

[70] Beth Understahl, "Authorized Generics: Careful Balance Undone," 16 Fordham Intellectual Property, Media, and Entertainment Law Journal (Autumn 2005), 355.

[71] Tony Pugh, "Loophole May Dampen Generic-drug Boom," San Jose Mercury News, May 3, 2006, A1.

[72] David A. Balto, "We'll Sell Generics Too: Innovator Drug Makers are Gaming the Regulatory System and Harming Competition," Legal Times, March 20, 2006.

[73] Jenna Greene, "The Drug Industry Has Figured Out a Way to Best Generic Competition, and Pharmaceutical Patent Litigation Could Free-Fall," New Jersey Law Journal, January 23, 2006, 217.

[74] See Pugh, supra note 54.

[75] Narinder Banait, "Authorized Generics: Antitrust Issues and the Hatch-Waxman Act," Mondaq, November 4, 2005.

[76] Virtual Patent Extension by Cannibalization.

[77] U.S. Food and Drug Administration, FDA Supports Broader Access to Lower Priced Drugs, FDA Talk Paper, July 2, 2004. A study prepared by IMS Consulting for the Pharmaceutical Research and Manufacturers of America reached a similar conclusion, determining that the average price discount to brand name drugs during the 180-day exclusivity period is greater when an authorized generic has been marketed than when one has not. IMS Consulting, Assessment of Authorized Generics in the U.S., Spring 2006, available at http://www.phrma.org/files/ IMS%20Authorized%20Generics%20Report_6-22-06.pdf.

[78] Kathleen Kerr, "Prescription Hurdles: Need Brand-Name Drug? Generic May Come First," Newsday, March 16, 2006, B13.

[79] Jon Hess and Elio Evangelista, Authorized Generics: Lifecycle Management's Compromise in the Patent Wars, Cutting Edge Information, August 23, 2005, 4.

[80] Ibid.

[81] James Bessen and Michael J. Meurer, "Lessons for Patent Policy from Empirical Research on Patent Litigation," Lewis and Clark Law Review, 2005.

[82] Christopher Worrell, Authorized Generics, presentation given at The 5th Generic Drugs Summit, September 27-29, 2004, and David Reiffen and Michael R. Ward, "Branded Generics" as a Strategy to Limit Cannibalization of Pharmaceutical Markets, May 2005, 2-4 available at http://www.uta.edu/faculty/mikeward/brandedgenerics.pdf.

[83] See CRS Report RL33717, Pharmaceutical Patent Litigation Settlements: Implications for Competition and Innovation, by John R. Thomas.

[84] Herbert Hovenkamp et al., "Anticompetitive Settlement of Intellectual Property Disputes," Minnesota Law Review, 2003, 1719.

[85] Ibid at 1764, n.196.

[86] In re Cardizem CD Antitrust Litigation, 332 F.3d 896 (6th Cir. 2003) ("reverse payment" settlement constitutes a per se illegal restraint of trade under section 1 of the Sherman Act).

[87] Valley Drug Co. v. Geneva Pharms., 344 F.3d 1294 (Fed. Cir. 2003) ("reverse payment" settlement not per se unlawful under section 1 of the Sherman Act).

[88] Neal R. Stoll & Shepard Goldfein, "Patent Protection or Per Se Violation?," New York Law Journal, Nov. 18, 2003, 3.

[89] For a detailed discussion of this issue see CRS Report R41483, Follow-On Biologics: The Law and Intellectual Property Issues, by Wendy H. Schacht and John R. Thomas.

[90] The Public Health Service defines the term "biological product" to mean "a virus, therapeutic serum, toxin, antitoxin, vaccine, blood, blood component or derivative, allergenic product, or analogous product, or arsphenamine or derivative of arsphenamine (or any other trivalent

organic arsenic compound), applicable to the prevention, treatment, or cure of a disease or condition of human beings." 42 U.S.C. §262(i) (2006).

[91] Beyond Borders, Global Biotechnology Report 2008, 30.

[92] Kerry A. Dolan, "Biology Rising," Forbes.com, May 12, 2006, available at http://www. forbes.com/2006/05/12/ merck-pfizer-amgen-cz_kd_0512biologics_print.html.

[93] "Biogenerics: A Difficult Birth?" IMS Global Insights, available at http://www. imshealth. com.

[94] Parexel Consulting, Follow-on Biologics, available at http://www.parexelconsulting.com/ services/follow-onbiologics.html

[95] FierceBiotech, The Top 10 Biosimilar Players: Positioning, performance and SWOT analyses, April 20, 2009, available at http://www.fiercebiotech.com/research/top-10-biosimilar-players-positioning-performance-and-swotanalyses.

[96] PriceWaterhouseCoopers, Biotech, Lifting Big Pharma's prospects with biologics, 2009, 9, available at http://www.pwc.com/en_GX/gx/pharma-life-sciences/pdf/biotech-final.pdf

[97] David M. Dudzinski, "Reflections on Historical, Scientific, and Legal Issues Relevant to Designing Approval Pathways for Generic Versions of Recombinant Protein-Based Therapeutics and Monoclonal Antibodies,"Food and Drug Law Journal, 2005, 143.

[98] Melissa R. Leuenberger-Fisher, "The Road to Follow On Biologics: Are We There Yet?," Biotechnology Law Report, August 2004, 389.

[99] Dawn Willow, "The Regulation of Biologic Medicine: Innovators' Rights and Access to Healthcare," Chicago-Kent Journal of Intellectual Property, 2006, 32.

[100] Ibid.

[101] See Dudzinski, supra (noting such concerns).

[102] Narinder S. Banait, Follow-on Biological Products—Legal Issues, 2005, available at http://www.fenwick.com/ docstore/Publications/IP/follow-on.pdf.

[103] For a detailed discussion of this legislation see CRS Report R41483, Follow-On Biologics: The Law and Intellectual Property Issues, by Wendy H. Schacht and John R. Thomas.

INDEX

M

N

O

P

R

S

T